Amazing Moms!
Motherhood
Curriculum

Amazing Moms! Motherhood Curriculum

Dr. Sophia Murphy, DBH, LPC

Dan Griffin, MA

Harrison Crawford, LPC, LIAC

WILEY

Published by John Wiley & Sons, Inc., Hoboken, New Jersey.
Published simultaneously in Canada.

For general information on our other products and services or for technical support, please contact our Customer Care Department within the United States at (800) 762-2974, outside the United States at (317) 572-3993 or fax (317) 572-4002.

Wiley also publishes its books in a variety of electronic formats. Some content that appears in print may not be available in electronic formats. For more information about Wiley products, visit our web site at www.wiley.com.

Library of Congress Cataloging-in-Publication Data Applied for:

Set ISBN: 9781394330836

Workbook: 9781394304349

Cover Design: Wiley
Cover Image: © Sofimanning/Shutterstock

Set in 11/16pt Palatino by Straive, Pondicherry, India

SKY10125697_090525

CONTENTS

About the Amazing Moms! *Program   vii*
About This Workbook   xi

Meeting   1: Engaging the Mother Within   1

Meeting   2: The Woman Rules   11

Meeting   3: Toxic Water   17

Meeting   4: Cultivating an Intrapersonal Relationship of Compassion   23

Meeting   4.5: Assaults on Our Bodies and Minds   33

Meeting   5: Moms and Trauma: Breaking the Cycle   41

Meeting   6: Making the Connections – Mental Health, Addiction, and Trauma   53

Meeting   7: Feelings… Nothing More Than Feelings   69

Meeting   8: Exploring Family Dynamics, Past and Present   81

Meeting   9: Father of Mine   89

Meeting   10: Mothers   99

Meeting   11: Healthy Relationships – Boundaries, Communication, and Conflict   107

Meeting   12: Let's Talk About Sex   119

Meeting   13: Let's REALLY Talk About Sex   129

Meeting   14: Women's Health   139

Meeting   15: Healthy Discipline   149

Meeting   16: The Art of Play   161

Meeting   17: A Balancing Act   167

Meeting   18: Vision of Motherhood   175

Congratulatory   181

Participant Survey   183

Appendix A: Relaxation and Grounding Exercises   185

References   195

CONTENTS

About the American Journal Program... xi

About the Workbook... xi

Meeting 1: Engaging the Mother Within... 1

Meeting 2: The Mother Wound... 11

Meeting 3: Toxic Worth... 19

Meeting 4: Cultivating an Interpersonal Relationship of Compassion... 23

Meeting 5: Issues on Internalizing and Mask... 35

Meeting 5: Shame and Trauma: Breaking the Cycle... 41

Meeting 6: Making the Connections: Mental Health, Addiction, and trauma... 53

Meeting 7: Feelings: Notice... More than Feelings... 55

Meeting 8: Knowing, Honoring Ourselves: Past and Present... 81

Meeting 9: Father of Mine...

Meeting 10: Mothers... 90

Meeting 11: Healthy Relationships: Boundaries, Communication, Trust, and Conflict... 101

Meeting 12: Let's Talk About Sex... 119

Meeting 13: Let's REALLY Talk About Sex... 129

Meeting 14: Women's Health... 139

Meeting 15: Healthy Discipline... 149

Meeting 16: The Artful Blay... 161

Meeting 17: A Different Act... 162

Meeting 18: Visions of Motherhood... 175

Conclusion... 181

Autobiographical Survey... 183

Appendix A: Relaxation and Grounding Exercises... 185

References... 195

ABOUT THE *AMAZING MOMS!* PROGRAM

Congratulations on starting the *Amazing Moms!* program. Our guess is that you are already *amazing*! Our hope is that you will find tools in this program that will allow you to be even more *amazing* and maybe even confirm for yourself just how *amazing* you are.

Amazing Moms![1] is a program unlike any other. While there are numerous outstanding programs and curricula for moms, only a minority appear to specifically address trauma and none of them seem to fully address the implications of female socialization on the moms. There appears to be no other motherhood curriculum that is based on the principles of female-responsive trauma-informed care like *Amazing Dads!* is the partner curriculum that this one is modeled after and is the first trauma-informed curriculum for Dads The goal of this program is to help you develop an informed and intentional vision of *both* the woman and mother you want to be.

It is important to recognize that as a mother, you have different needs, face different challenges, and want different guidance with parenting than fathers do. This program addresses that reality in a way that you will hopefully find both comforting in the way it speaks to you as a woman and a mother and challenging in that you will be asked to do a great deal of self-reflection. The goal of *Amazing Moms!* is to help you create a vision of the mother you want to be and to provide you with the awareness, tools, and confidence to achieve that vision.

This program is designed to be trauma-informed. That means that the language, activities, and tools throughout the program are meant to be challenging but in a way that is safe. Everything in the program was designed with an assumption that all participants have experienced some level or form of trauma in their lives, and creating

---

[1] The terms "mom" and "mother" are used to include all persons who identify as female, feminine, femme, and other identities that do not align with masculinity or the terms "dad" or "father." The goal is to use research around female socialization in Western Society to explore positive and negative consequences of being raised as a female or presenting as feminine and the impact that has on being a mother. This verbiage does not solely recognize gender as binary and is intended only as a means of context. The terms "woman," "women," and "female" will be used throughout for the same purpose.

an environment of safety for all participating moms was a top priority when creating the program. Trust and safety are key to creating lasting changes and becoming the mother you want to be. Whether you have experienced trauma in your life or not, the trauma-informed approach is designed to create a safe environment for you to do the work that will help you become the mother you want to be.

You are reading this because you have decided to make (or are considering making) fundamental changes in how you show up as a mother. In most cases, you will be using this workbook as part of a program in which you meet regularly with a group of other mothers. As part of this process, you will attend 19 meetings with these other mothers and all of you will have opportunities to develop new skills and new ways of thinking about yourself, your children, your families, and motherhood. One of the most powerful aspects of this program is the group setting where you will get to see just how common many of the issues are that mothers face but also to explore important differences that make each mother unique and able to offer diverse perspectives. Again, the organization of the program is designed to make this group setting safe and trusting in a way that many mothers have not had the fortune of experiencing.

Topics covered in this program include:

- The impact of female socialization on girls, women, and mothers (a core theme that guides the whole curriculum).
- Trauma, how it shows up in women and mothers, and the importance of addressing any trauma history you might have.
- Skill-building and practical tools you can use with, and teach to, your children.
- Relationship skill development.
- Developing emotional understanding, particularly as relates to anger and shame.
- Enhanced communication skills for healthy conflict resolution.
- The influence of family of origin experiences.
- Exploring the relationships with mothers/mother figures and fathers/ father figures.
- A candid exploration of sex, sexuality, and intimacy and how to begin having a healthy dialogue about these topics with your children.
- Differentiating discipline from punishment, understanding how punishment can turn into abuse, and identifying what healthy discipline looks like.
- The effects of female socialization on your ability to create and maintain healthy relationships, offering specific tools to help repair during times of disconnection.

- Finding balance and the importance of self-care as part of being a healthy mother.
- Understanding and meeting the changing roles and expectations of women and mothers in the twenty-first century.

The hope is that your exploration of all these topics and your experiences will help you develop an idea of the mother you want to be, whether that be confirming that you are already showing up in ways that align with the mother you want to be, or identifying some changes you want to make to help align yourself with that vision of the mother you want to be. You can always check out the *Amazing Moms!* website at www.amazing-moms.com for more information and resources.

ABOUT THIS WORKBOOK

This workbook is meant for you to be able to record your experiences throughout this program. Using this workbook will help you reflect on and remember what you learn, think, and feel during the group meetings and as you continue to practice the tools you learn on your own between meetings. The workbook contains:

- Summaries of information you will receive in the group meetings.
- Many of the activities and exercises that you will do during the group meetings.
- Activities for you to work on between the group meetings.
- Space for you to reflect on what you learned in each meeting.
- A section where all the grounding and relaxation exercises are listed so you have easy access to them whenever you might want to use one or refresh your memory of them.

The activities that are to be completed between the group meetings are designed to help you reflect on what you have learned and to put some new skills and behaviors into practice. The "Into Action" exercises are meant to help you put what was discussed in the meeting directly into action in your own life. There are also additional Practical and Tactical exercises designed as deeper dives into the material and information discussed in the meetings. These are meant to be optional, additional ways you can explore the discussions and reflect on your own experiences.

Often people learn best by doing, and these activities also help you see the benefits of what you are practicing. The activities are not things you have to do to pass a class. Some of them involve writing or drawing exercises, but your skills in these areas are not being tested. You do not need to worry about your handwriting or spelling. What matters is what you put into the activities and, consequently, what you get out of them. There are no right or wrong answers, no "shoulds" or "shouldn'ts," and your work will not be checked or graded. This workbook is a tool to help you with your growth toward the vision of the mother you want to be, and something you can keep and look back on in the future to remind you of your growth and to use as a resource for things like grounding and relaxation exercises you will learn.

There will be opportunities during some of the group meetings for you to share what you have written in your workbook. You can share what you want and keep the rest private. The group meeting is a safe place, and there will be ground rules regarding confidentiality. If writing is difficult for you that is okay, you can draw pictures or simply make notes however works best for you.

You can use this workbook to highlight what you want to remember from each meeting and to make notes about what you are thinking and feeling as you go through this program.

You may be concerned about keeping your workbook private. If you live with others and are not sure they will respect your privacy, you should hide your workbook or lock it up. Or you can ask the facilitator or another trusted person to help you find a way to keep your workbook safe between group meetings. The facilitator is prepared for such requests. If the facilitator will be holding your workbook between meetings, he or she will respect your privacy and arrange for you to complete the extra activities after each meeting or at some other time.

MEETING 1

Engaging the Mother Within

Welcome! Congratulations on making the decision to work toward becoming the best mother you can be. This is your first step toward becoming the Amazing Mom you have inside. Your first meeting in the *Amazing Moms!* program is an introduction to what you can expect throughout your participation in the meetings. There is a discussion of the different goals of the program, and then you will have opportunities to explore your own goals for your time in the program as well as some important questions about what motherhood means to you. This meeting is meant to "set the stage" for the rest of the program.

The goals of Meeting 1 are:

1. To discuss the structure of the program.
2. To go over the group agreements and expectations.
3. To explore what motherhood means to you.
4. To commit to putting in the work to be the mother you want to be.

Amazing Moms! Motherhood Curriculum, Workbook, First Edition. Sophia Murphy, Dan Griffin, and Harrison Crawford.
© 2026 Sophia Murphy, Dan Griffin, and Harrison Crawford. Published 2026 by John Wiley & Sons, Inc.

Group Agreements

At the beginning of Meeting 1, your facilitator will explain some group agreements that will be maintained during each of the group meetings. Part of creating an environment of safety and trust in the program and with one another comes from each mother committing to follow these agreements. The group agreements listed here are the common ones that are recommended, but the ones in your group may differ if there are specific requirements that the facilitator needs to follow.

Safety

You agree to help create a safe space for everyone. This means physical safety, as well as a feeling of safety where each mom can share her experiences, opinions, and thoughts without fear of being shamed. You agree there will be no physical or verbal abuse. You agree to discuss any concerns for safety with the group facilitator(s).

Attendance and Participation

You agree to attend all meetings. If a conflict keeps you from being able to attend, you agree to contact the facilitator(s) ahead of time. You also commit to choosing to be on time for each meeting. You agree to participate and stretch outside our comfort zone as best you can, even if it is challenging. Also, each participant has a right to decide something is too uncomfortable to share and you agree to respect each mom's right to decide that for herself. You agree to keep focused on the topics of each meeting. You agree to help each other stay focused, including helping the facilitator(s) stay on topic.

Confidentiality

You agree to keep everything that is said in this group, in this group. You will not discuss the experiences or information shared by other moms outside this group. All participants are responsible for keeping confidentiality in the group. You understand that any limits to confidentiality on the part of the facilitator(s) will be explained to you as appropriate.

Respect

You agree to respect all participants and facilitators – their time, their experiences, and their challenges. You do not have to agree all the time, but when you disagree, you will do so while respecting the other's experience. You agree to share the time in this group, showing others respect by allowing each mom opportunities to share and participate. You agree to show respect by being honest when you choose to share as well as when you give feedback to others.

Other (feel free to write any others that your facilitator or group identifies here):

There are times in this group when you likely will feel uncomfortable or anxious. This happens to all of us at various times, especially in unfamiliar settings and with new experiences. As a woman, you were likely taught to keep these feelings to yourself. Women are often taught from a young age to avoid seeming "dramatic" or to draw to much attention to themselves for being "too emotional." As a result, when you experience discomfort, you might not know how to deal with it in healthy ways. Throughout your time in this program, you will learn many different techniques that you can use to help you relax, calm yourself, and feel more grounded. The first two techniques (the ones you learned in Meeting 1) are listed next. There is also an Appendix at the back of this workbook where all the techniques are available for your reference later.

Box Breathing

This exercise can help you calm your body and your mind quickly and efficiently:

1. Put one hand on your chest and the other on your stomach.
2. As you take a few breaths, notice which hand is moving more. Try moving your breath deeper into your lower abdomen, so that your hand on your stomach moves more as you breathe.
3. Close your mouth and press your tongue lightly to the roof of your mouth. Let your jaw relax.
4. Take in a full breath slowly through your nose, counting to four.
5. Hold your breath, counting to four.
6. Exhale all the air through your mouth, counting to four.
7. Rest for a count of four.
8. As thoughts come up, acknowledge them, and then return your focus to your breathing and counting.
9. Go through three more rounds of this breathing on your own, slowly breathing in through your nose for four counts, holding for four counts, breathing out through your mouth for four counts, and resting for four counts.

Deep breathing can be helpful when dealing with feelings of anger, stress, fear, panic, or any other uncomfortable feelings. Plus, it is generally healthier to take controlled, deep breaths versus shallow ones. The more you practice this way of breathing, the more natural it will become for you.

Palms Up, Palms Down

This exercise can help you move aside anything that is weighing on your mind, or even any physical discomfort, to allow you to focus your mind on the present.

1. Sit up straight in your seat, with both feet on the floor and your eyes focused on your hands.
2. Hold both your arms outstretched, with your palms side by side and facing up as if someone was about to put something in your hands. Make sure you don't rest your arms on anything; they should be out in front of you in the air.
3. Visualize any thoughts, feelings, and stresses bothering you right now.
4. Now imagine placing all of your stresses, problems, troubles, and anything bothering you into your hands. These emotions and thoughts are out of your bodies and lying in your hands. Picture them there.
5. Go back inside yourself and find any remaining pain, discomfort, and stress. Then feel these sensations slowly move through your arms and into your hands.
6. Imagine the weight of holding all these problems, difficult thoughts and emotions, and physical distress in your hands. Feel the strain of carrying them and the weight pushing down on your hands.
7. Now, slowly turn your hands upside down letting your palms face the floor. Let all the problems, stresses, difficult feelings, and negativity fall to the floor. For now, drop your burdens.

All these problems have not disappeared or been resolved, but you have chosen to put them down for the time being to be able to focus on what you need to.

Consider practicing Box Breathing and Palms Up, Palms Down exercises between meetings. Like any new skill, the more you practice these exercises, the more efficient you will get at using them and the more effective they can be at helping you calm your body and your mind.

A big part of the *Amazing Moms!* program is building a vision of the mother you want to be and the ways you want to show up for your kids and as a mother. One of the first exercises is to begin thinking about what you want to get out of going through this program. Whether you have been told you need to go through this program or you are participating voluntarily, you have an opportunity to think about what you can get out of this experience to help you as a mother.

Expectations – What Do You Want to Get Out of This Group?

There may be many reasons you chose to use this workbook and participate in this program. Whatever brought you to *Amazing Moms!*, it is important to consider what you want to gain from your participation. Consider what you want to get out of your time doing this important work and how you want to use this opportunity to become the mother you want to be.

What is the work that you are here to do to become the best mother you can be?

What are some things you would like to learn through this process?

What Is Motherhood to You?

You may not have had an opportunity to think about this before. It may sound like a simple thought, but there is value in taking some time to answer the following questions:

1. What does motherhood mean to you?

2. What does being a mom mean to you?

3. What are some of the positives of being involved as a mom? Think about positives for you and positives for your children.

4. What is one of the toughest parts of being a mom?

5. What do you enjoy most about being a mom?

Commitment to Conscious Motherhood

"I commit to practicing what I learn. I will do my best to let go of wanting to do this perfectly. Instead, I will consciously practice being the best mother I can be."

This commitment is incredibly important to your growth as a mother. It shows that you are willing to try new things with an open mind. It also means that you agree to be kind to yourself and give yourself grace in your efforts. This is not about perfection but rather using the things you learn in a conscious way, making purposeful choices about how you show up as a mom.

Next, you will find the first Into Action and Practical & Tactical exercises from Meeting 1. These exercises appear at the end of each meeting and are meant to be completed between meetings to practice parts of what was covered. The Practical & Tactical exercises are a chance to do a deeper dive into what was discussed in each meeting.

Into Action: Values Clarification – What Is Important to You?

Part of being the best mom you can be is thinking about what you personally find important – your values – and making a conscious decision to act in ways to live by those values. Just as importantly, you will want to act in ways that align with your values in order to pass those values down to your children.

Look at the list of possible values on this page. Take a few minutes to read through all of them and pick your top 10. Number your top 10, with number 1 being the most important to you. Feel free to identify any values you hold that are not on the list, using the blank spaces provided.

Love	Wealth	Respect
Family	Morals	Stability
Success	Knowledge	Fairness
Power	Friends	Relaxation
Free time	Adventure	Peace
Variety	Calmness	Wisdom
Freedom	Fun	Creativity
Recognition	Nature	Safety
Popularity	Responsibility	Beauty
Honesty	Humor	Spirituality
Loyalty	Reason	Independence
Achievement		

Please answer the following questions:

1. The values I *would like* to live by are…

2. The values I *actually* live by are…

3. The values I would like my children to learn from me are…

4. Three things I can do to promote these values to my children are…

   a.

   b.

   c.

Hopefully, you have a clearer picture of the values you find important and want to instill in your children.

Next is the first Practical & Tactical exercise. These exercises or activities are also meant to be completed between meetings. They offer opportunities to explore the topics discussed in the meetings on a deeper level to help you continue to take on the information you learned in each meeting.

Practical & Tactical

Have a conversation with your children about what you value and what is important to you. This conversation can vary based on the age of your children, but share what you learned about yourself and your values in the assignment with your children. Have this conversation with your partner, coparent, a family member, or a trusted friend as well.

Ask your children about their values. Even at a young age, teaching a child to be aware of what is important to him or her is a helpful exercise.

Summary

Congratulations on your commitment to becoming the best mother you can be!

After participating in this first meeting, you should have a better sense of what to expect from the *Amazing Moms!* program. You spent time discussing some group agreements that will help everyone create a group that is safe, open to different ideas and opinions, where you are accountable to yourself and your fellow moms, and they are accountable to you in return.

You also learned three different grounding and relaxation exercises: Box Breathing, Palms Up/Palms Down, and In With The Good Breathing. You will have many opportunities to practice these during the upcoming meetings, plus you will learn even more throughout the rest of the program. The hope is that you will continue to build your toolbox of skills to feel more confident in your ability to care for yourself in times of distress. Remember, there is a section at the back of this workbook where you can find all the exercises you will learn, so you can easily find whatever you may need.

Throughout your time in this program, you will learn many skills, be exposed to new ideas, and have many opportunities to think about and practice how you might use this new information in your life and with your children. Please keep in mind that the goal is not using everything you learn perfectly, but rather being more conscious and intentional about your choices. You will make mistakes, and it is okay. Congratulations on taking the first step toward becoming an Amazing Mom!

MEETING 2

The Woman Rules

While all meetings in this program are important, this meeting is one that sets the stage for the entire *Amazing Moms!* program. In this meeting, you will learn how the ways that girls are raised make a huge impact on how they see the world, how they see what is safe for them or not, and how they relate to others in their lives. You will discuss how many of the "rules" for girls and women are often pressed upon them in harmful ways and how those rules push girls and women away from healthy connections with others.

The result is that many girls and women feel safer when they stick to rules that are actually harmful to them. All of this has a big impact on how you show up as a mother, whether you realize it now or not.

The goals of Meeting 2 are:

1. To better understand your ideas about femininity and being a woman.
2. To better understand the qualities of healthy mothering.
3. To look at typical messages about being a woman and how they help or harm your experience of being a mother.

Amazing Moms! Motherhood Curriculum, Workbook, First Edition. Sophia Murphy, Dan Griffin, and Harrison Crawford.
© 2026 Sophia Murphy, Dan Griffin, and Harrison Crawford. Published 2026 by John Wiley & Sons, Inc.

Part of the opening for each meeting moving forward will include the "Feelings and Body Check-In." This is a way to begin recognizing your own emotional state in the moment, which is something many moms are not used to thinking about. To help you identify new feeling words, you will find an image of the "Feelings Wheel" below that lists many feeling words that you can choose from while expanding your emotional vocabulary.

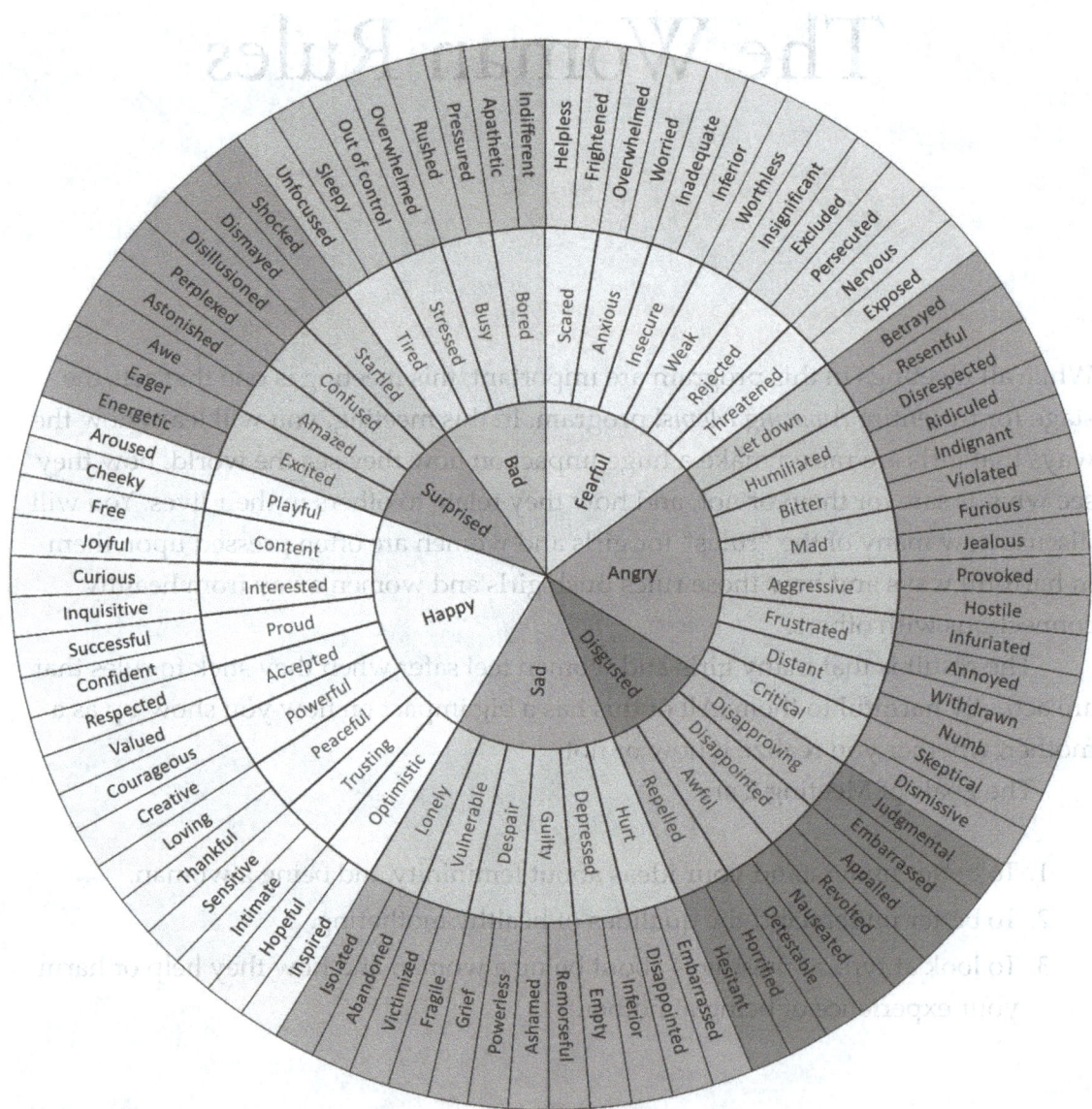

The Feelings Wheel retrieved from: https://feelingswheel.com/

Important Concept: The Water

There is one concept that informs almost everything we are going to discuss in this program. That concept is called "The Water." A good way to describe this concept is through a brief story: There are two young fish swimming along, and another fish swims up to them and says, "Hey guys, how's the water?" That fish smiles and then swims away. The two young fish swim along for a minute and then one looks at the other and says, "What the hell is water?"

The Water is our reality, and it is all around us. We are *IN* the Water. But, just like the two fish in the story, we don't even know the Water exists. It's just our experience of the world – we don't know anything different. And yet, the Water impacts us every single day in most of the ways we think and act.

One of the deepest parts of the Water is gender.

The Woman Rules

The next activity asks you to consider the rules about what it means to be a "real" woman. Not all the Woman Rules are negative or harmful. However, there are many that are, especially when they are pushed to the extreme or clung to rigidly. Many of them limit women and moms, encouraging hyperfocus on others, disconnection from the self, and a false belief in the need for women and moms to be perfect. The Woman Rules activity will help you identify the rules as you experience them as well as how they do or do not line up with your ideas about what it means to be a healthy mother.

- What are the "rules" for being a woman?

This next activity has you explore what it takes to be a healthy mother. What types of expectations, behaviors, and so on are needed to be able to be a healthy mother? When we say "healthy," this is not the same as "good" and is rather about moving more and more toward being a conscious mother. In other words, when you imagine being a healthy mother, what are you doing? How are you interacting with your children?

The Components of Healthy Mothering

- What are the components of being a healthy mother?

Subgroup Discussion: The Woman Rules vs. Healthy Mothering

Now that you have explored the Woman Rules and the components of what it means to be a healthy mother, please answer the following questions in your subgroup.

- Which of the Woman Rules *support* being a healthy mother?

- Which of the Woman Rules *do not support* being a healthy mother?

You spent this meeting considering what "rules" you learned about femininity growing up and how they do or do not line up with the skills it takes to be a healthy mother. After each meeting, you will be invited to explore some additional activities that will help you use this information in your life outside of the group. Please take some time to complete the following activities before your next meeting.

Into Action: The Woman Rules and Healthy Mothering

Part 1: Choose three of the Woman Rules that you can relate to, and that *support* being a healthy mother. Write about how those Rules have helped you as a mother. Share what you have written with your partner or a trusted friend.

Part 2: Choose three of the Woman Rules that you can relate to, but that *do not support* healthy mothering. Write about how those rules have hindered you as a mother. What are three ways you can do things differently when it comes to these rules, so that they have less of an impact on you? Share what you have written with your partner or a trusted friend.

Practical & Tactical

Write out a list of Woman Rules or Man Rules (depending on the gender of your child or children) you are comfortable exploring with your children. Discuss these rules with them. Give them the opportunity to learn about what the rules are and where they come from to become more conscious of them and to choose what is best for them. Give them the choice that you were not given. After you have the discussion, write a little about what it was like, what went well, and what didn't. If your child identifies as non-binary or trans have a conversation with them about gender and what it's like for them going against the main rules of our society. Look for an opportunity to connect regarding the pain that you both be able to identify regarding gender. If you are not comfortable having this discussion with them, write down ways you can consciously act and model the rules you want them to learn from you. If applicable, discuss this with your partner, significant other, or coparent.

Summary

After finishing this meeting, it should be clear that much of what we believe about femininity and what being a "real" woman really means comes from our upbringing and the messages we got from parents, teachers, peers, coaches, and the media. This is true for all people, but for girls and women, it often turns out to be damaging because many of the messages we receive are often unhealthy and "taught" to us in ways that are harmful.

As you start to recognize what messages and Woman Rules you absorbed, you now have an opportunity to decide for yourself what you do with that knowledge. We encourage you to use this new awareness to help you make decisions about how you want to show up as a woman and as a mother. You likely did not have a choice about what Woman Rules were impressed upon you, but the beauty of learning about this is that you now have the choice about how you move forward. Even more importantly, you now have better information to influence how your kids grow and learn about these rules, both the positive ones and the more harmful ones.

It is important to remember that the goal in using this new information is not that you will use it perfectly and make only the "right" choices all the time. Rather, the goal is to use this information and be conscious of what influences you so you can change your thinking, change your actions, and become the mother you want to be. This is what is called conscious femininity and conscious motherhood, and you have taken another important step forward on this journey.

MEETING 3

Toxic Water

This meeting continues with the theme of the Water, highlighting many ways culture strongly influences how we understand the world around us. This is especially true when it comes to how we perceive others, specifically people who are different from us. It is important to explore these ideas for multiple reasons: to begin thinking about how your own culture fits (or doesn't fit) into the larger system, to get honest about the ideas, beliefs, and judgments you have internalized about other people and groups, to imagine ways you can use your culture to create more equality and understanding among the people in your lives, and to consider how you can help your children see their own power in celebrating differences and recognizing the value of diversity.

The goals of Meeting 3 are:

1. To better understand the systemic impact of patriarchy and the toxic culture of masculinity as they relate to the trauma that women can experience and perpetuate.
2. To better understand how the unique experiences of trauma are influenced by the intersection of culture, race, class, and gender.
3. To explore how privilege and entitlement create disconnection and harm in your relationships and your communities, and to highlight how to use this awareness to make positive changes personally and for your children.

Amazing Moms! Motherhood Curriculum, Workbook, First Edition. Sophia Murphy, Dan Griffin, and Harrison Crawford.

Skills for being able to imagine what someone else is going through are desperately needed in order to have a positive impact on others and on the world. Being able to imagine someone else's experience and feelings is called empathy. You cannot be a conscious mother without learning how to have true empathy for your children. Building empathy is something you can promote in your children, and it starts with being able to put yourself "in the shoes" of someone else. This next activity focuses on being able to do that.

Important Concept: The Toxins in The Water

The ways we raise boys to be men and girls to be women is what we call gender conditioning. Gender conditioning is a huge part of the Water and in all honesty, it is part of what *poisons* the Water. It is important to remember that not all the Woman Rules are bad. There are many aspects of femininity that can be quite positive. But the truth is not all girls and women are socialized in the same ways. The Water in which we all swim is filled with toxins, but the toxins affect each of us differently.

We live in a patriarchal society that favors men over women and a society of white privilege that favors the white experience, especially the middle- and upper-class white experience, over other lived experiences. Beyond that there are systems of power that have been set up that have used systemic violence and discrimination to prevent various groups from having full and equal access to our society and its resources. The effects of this violence have impacted many communities and generations of families for centuries, causing generational trauma that many people of privilege are often not aware of and may even dismiss.

This is still happening today even if we have made a lot of progress. Black, Indigenous, and People of Color, also known as BIPOC, have more representation politically and in the corporate world as well as greater representation in media than ever before. However, the recent conversations around police violence, racially motivated attacks, the growing voice of white supremacist groups, the disproportionate removal of children of color from their homes, and other issues remind us that we have a long way to go in this country.

So, if you are in this group and you are not white, it is important that this is a safe place for you and that there is space for your voice, your experiences, *and your pain* that can be different from what others have experienced. It is likely that you have had, or will have, different conversations with your children about how to navigate the world depending on the characteristics you and your children possess. For example, non-white individuals often have very different conversations with their children when it comes to police. It is important to acknowledge the effect this has.

We also live in a society that says "normal" is heterosexual and that gender must be masculine or feminine which is a term called binarism. It's true that due to many more gay and lesbian individuals having positions of power and influence, there is some acceptance of a sexual identity that is not heterosexual. But in some geographic, religious, and political spheres, there is still a lot of discrimination, oppression, and even hatred toward individuals and groups who don't fall into their concept or "normal."

What does this have to do with your being a mother? This exploration can create opportunities to heal trauma you may be carrying from your experiences, but also opportunities to better understand and communicate these important ideas to your children. Your conversations with your children will differ depending on your characteristics and experiences, but no matter what, the benefit of being able to have these open conversations with your children is that you can be a model for them. This is an opportunity to help break the cycle of trauma resulting from generations of systemic inequality and abuse.

If you can begin to see the privilege that you have, please consider how you might use that privilege to make a difference to others. Could you even be a voice for those who do not have the same opportunities, power, or privilege that you have? Whether it is addressing the discrimination and prejudice that your kids may experience and need to be able to talk about, or it is the discrimination and prejudice that your kids may witness, it is vital that you have open channels for communication with your kids about these topics. Modeling for your kids can help them gain a deeper understanding of their own experiences and even create positive change.

Subgroup Discussion: The Shoes of Another

Based on the description you received on the slip of paper you were given, take some time to answer the following questions in your small group. There is space for you to take notes if you choose to.

1. What messages do you believe a child who fits this description has gotten from society?

2. In what ways, if any, do you think the messages changed as this person grew into an adult?

3. What kind of challenging experiences do you think this person may have had based solely on their characteristics?

4. What kind of messages do you believe this person has to share with their children about their identity and place in our society?

Now that you have spent time empathizing with someone very different from yourself, take some time to reflect on your own lived experiences by answering the following questions in your small group.

1. What kind of messages did you *receive* about your own identity from society as a child?

2. What kind of *healthy* messages do you *send yourself* about your identity?

3. What kind of *unhealthy* messages do you *send yourself* about your identity?

4. What kind of challenging experiences have you had *as a mother* based on your personal characteristics?

5. What kind of challenging experiences have *your children* endured because of their personal characteristics?

Building empathy in yourself and in your children is one way to "cleanse the toxic water" that we all encounter. Healing can begin when people try to understand one another and empathize with each other's experiences.

Into Action: Reflections on Toxic Water

Please take some time to answer the following questions:

1. What messages did your parent(s) or caregiver(s) pass on to you regarding your identity and cultural characteristics?

2. What messages did you get from society about your identity and cultural characteristics?

3. What do you want your children to know about their own identity and cultural characteristics? Are they similar to what your parent(s) or caregiver(s) taught you? Are they different? Why?

4. How did you (or will you) respond to your children asking questions about their identity, culture, or privilege?

Practical & Tactical

In order to explore this subject even further, you are invited to have a conversation about these topics with one person in your life that you have never spoken to about this – a best friend, parent, mentor, other family members, etc. You are encouraged to share any insights you gained from the meeting, what you feel about what was discussed, anything that stood out to you as important, and to ask the person you choose to talk to about her/his own thoughts on this information.

Summary

During this meeting, you were introduced to the idea of Toxic Water. This refers to the biases, negative associations, and power imbalances that exist in our culture as part of the Water. Much of this program is about building awareness of things you may not have known before beginning this journey. This meeting focused on building awareness of the cultural and societal influences you and others experience and, depending on your own background, may negatively impact you and your children. This is not an easy discussion to have, so please remember to take care of yourself by practicing any or all of the breathing and grounding exercises you have learned so far.

Cultivating an Intrapersonal Relationship of Compassion

This meeting brings your attention back to the Woman Rules and the significant impact they can have on your relationship with someone who often gets overlooked… you! You will start by considering the messages contained within the Woman Rules as well as the types of positive *and* negative messages you have internalized about what it means to be a woman. You then get the opportunity to explore the messages that you tell yourself and how they may impact your parenting, including the messages you send your child or children.

The goals of Meeting 4 are:

1. To understand the concept of the intrapersonal relationship (your connection to yourself).
2. To explore how a woman's identity is largely shaped only in relation to service to others and how this impacts the experience of motherhood.
3. To examine how women are taught to connect their self-worth to the evaluations from external factors.
4. To look at how healing trauma begins with healing the intrapersonal relationship in order to be the mother you want to be.

Amazing Moms! Motherhood Curriculum, Workbook, First Edition. Sophia Murphy, Dan Griffin, and Harrison Crawford.

The Woman Rules and Internal Messages

This is a brief review and reexamination of the Woman Rules and the messages that were passed along to you about being a "real" woman. You will also have the chance to explore the messages that you have been sending yourself to look at which Rules tend to show up consistently for you.

1. As a child, what kind of messages did you receive from society about being a woman?

2. What kind of *positive* messages do you send yourself about being a woman?

3. What kind of *negative* messages do you send yourself about being a woman?

Now, please think about how the messages you absorbed as part of the Woman Rules, and how those messages impact what you tell yourself and the ways in which you "talk" to yourself internally.

1. When was a time that you "fell short" on one of the Woman Rules and what did you tell yourself?

2. Think of a time that you behaved in a way that did not align with the Woman Rules or how you've come to believe a mother "should be." Describe it briefly below:

3. What was the outcome and how did it impact your self-talk?

4. How has your self-talk impacted the way you interact with your children?

Important Definition: Internal Messages

"The messages you think or say to yourself." These can also be referred to as your "self-talk."

Important Definition: Intrapersonal Relationship

"Your relationship to and with yourself."

As a woman and a mother, you are often encouraged to ignore your own needs and wants and focus on the needs and wants of others in your life, especially your children. However, being able to develop a healthy *intra*personal relationship can help you significantly in your relationships with others and act as a great model for your children.

Important Concept: "Don'ts" and "Bes" in Relationships

One of the most obvious parts of conscious motherhood is developing healthy relationships with those around you; however, you can't do that well without healing the relationship within. Most people follow the saying that, "you can't love someone else until you love yourself." While there is some truth to this, these two processes work together: Healing the *intra*personal relationship often leads to positive changes in the *inter*personal relationships - the relationships you have with others. The opposite can also be true: creating healthy *inter*personal relationships with others often helps you to heal the relationship with yourself.

The challenges women face with relationships come back to the Woman Rules. Our culture promotes a narrative that women, especially mothers, need to be selfless; that mothers can do it all and never need support from others. There definitely are some women who approach parenting and relationships that way. The Woman Rules are all about perfection, focusing on external evaluations from others, and denial of your own needs. Remember all of those "don'ts" you identified as part of the Rules? It is also important to remember the "Bes" and how the expectations of all the things women are "supposed to be" informs how they show up with others.

What is absent from the Woman Rules is the critical importance of connection to the self. A central theme of the Woman Rules is the development of relationships with others; however, that is based on the expectation of women to be purely selfless. The truth is that all human beings are hardwired for relationships and all human beings seek and find comfort in relationships. All human beings deserve to have their needs met without sacrificing themselves.

This highlights the importance of developing a healthy relationship with yourself because when you are disconnected in your relationship with *yourself*, you miss opportunities to get your needs met and care for yourself in healthy ways. However, having a healthy relationship with yourself isn't always so simple, especially if the intrapersonal relationship is negative, belittling, and critical. Building a strong connection to yourself involves first acknowledging the disconnect – verbally, physically, emotionally, spiritually – and consciously reconnecting with purpose and intention to mend or repair the relationship.

Subgroup Discussion: Early Childhood and The Woman Rules

Your exposure to the Woman Rules and messages about being a "real" girl and woman started at an early age. One of the first, and most unnoticed, ways those messages were communicated to you was through play. This next discussion will allow you to consider how play was likely a means of having the Woman Rules imposed on you. You will answer the following questions in your subgroup.

1. How were the Woman Rules introduced via play as a young girl?

2. How did the Woman Rules impact how you played and what you learned through play as a girl?

3. How do the Woman Rules impact how you play and what you play with your own children?

4. How does your body feel as you connect to these memories of your own childhood and as a mother now?

Creative Activity: The Mother Inside

The next activity will offer an opportunity to connect to yourself as a woman and a mother using your creativity. You are invited to create a drawing of yourself that includes all the different intersections you occupy. You are also encouraged to depict where in your body you hold stress and trauma related to those intersections and systems you find yourself in. Being able to recognize where your body holds these experiences, stressors, and traumas is a major step to becoming a more conscious mother. Awareness is the first step toward conscious choices about what to do next.

There is no "right" way to do this activity, only the way that speaks to you. You are invited to be as creative as you want in this activity. You'll find space on the next page for your drawing.

Creative Activity: The Mother Inside

Into Action

Please take some time to answer the following questions:

1. What messages (positive and negative) have you given your children about their relationship(s) with themselves and their bodies?

2. If your child expresses discomfort or distress with themselves (speaking critically, feeling low about themselves), how do you typically respond? Do you tend to minimize or tell them they are "fine," or do you ask questions? How might you be able to support their experience?

3. Based on our discussion in this meeting, what do you want your children to know about their relationships to themselves and their bodies? Are those messages you want them to know similar to what your parent(s) or caregiver(s) taught you? Are they different? How?

Practical & Tactical

Before the next meeting, please take some time to check in with your body. Set a timer for five minutes, find a quiet place, sit comfortably, and simply close your eyes and scan your body. Notice any physical discomfort you might be feeling as well as critical thoughts about yourself that may enter your mind. If being still is difficult or uncomfortable, simply notice that and do your best not to judge yourself. Try to repeat two to three times before the next meeting. You can record any notes or observations below.

Summary

As you discussed in today's meeting, the Woman Rules tend to push you towards disconnection from yourself and to deprioritize focusing on your intrapersonal relationship and your own self-care. This push toward disconnection starts at an early age, making it hard to even recognize by the time you become a mother. However, through your willingness to look at the Woman Rules and how they have impacted you, you have a new opportunity to make changes, if you so choose. The opportunity is there to recognize that *you* are important and that prioritizing your relationship with *yourself* is a valuable use of your time and energy. Plus, by practicing this yourself you can set the stage for your children. You can be a model for them to understand their own importance.

MEETING 4.5

Assaults on Our Bodies and Minds

This meeting will focus on a difficult topic, but one that cannot be avoided as part of a motherhood program: assaults on your physical body and your mind. You will learn the definitions of different terms that get used often but are not always clearly understood, like sexual assault and body autonomy. You will then learn how the combination of the Toxic Water, Woman Rules, and Man Rules all impact a woman's experience of violence, lack of body autonomy, and related traumas. The final activity of this meeting, though, brings you back to your internal sense of resilience and hope because you are invited to use your creativity to develop an artistic portrait of reclaiming your body autonomy. It may often feel like your autonomy has been taken from you, but you are encouraged to focus on your own resilience and power.

Please remember that you have tools available to you as you go through this material, especially the grounding and relaxation exercises you have learned and that are included at the end of this workbook (see the Appendix for all exercises).

The goals of Meeting 4.5 are:

1. To understand the commonplace experiences of rape and sexual assault for women.

2. To understand the nuanced challenges of pregnancy due to rape and the choices that follow (abortion/coerced abortion and the associated shame).

3. To explore the impact of violations on bodily autonomy on mothers.

4. To examine how women are taught to blame themselves and internalize the traumatic experiences of violations of their bodies.

5. To explore ways to heal through reclaiming your body autonomy.

Important Definitions: Sexual Assault and Rape

"The term sexual assault refers to sexual contact or behavior that occurs without explicit consent of the victim."

> – RAINN (Rape, Abuse & Incest National Network)
> www.rainn.org/articles/sexual-assault

"Rape is a form of sexual assault, but not all sexual assault is rape. The term rape is often used as a legal definition to specifically include sexual penetration without consent. For its Uniform Crime Reports, the FBI defines rape as 'penetration, no matter how slight, of the vagina or anus with any body part or object, or oral penetration by a sex organ of another person, without the consent of the victim.'"

> – RAINN (Rape, Abuse & Incest National Network)
> www.rainn.org/articles/sexual-assault

Important Concept: Rape Culture

"The attitudes and beliefs that perpetuate sexual violence… A culture that glamourizes violence against women, accepts misogynistic language, and generally accepts the belief that girls should impose limits on their own behavior to avoid getting raped is what lays the groundwork for rape culture."

> – Jennifer Shore, MA
> www.focusforhealth.org/rape-culture-in-america

Important Definition: Bodily Autonomy

"Bodily autonomy means that we have the power and agency to make choices over our bodies and futures, without violence or coercion. This includes when, whether or with whom to have sex. It includes when, whether or with whom you want to become pregnant. It means the freedom to go to a doctor whenever you need one."

> – UNFPA, the United Nations sexual and reproductive health agency.
> www.unfpa.org/sowp-2021/autonomy

The Woman Rules and Violations of Our Bodies

1. What aspects of the *Woman* Rules contribute to Rape Culture?

2. What aspects of the *Man* Rules contribute to Rape Culture?

3. What messages have you received regarding a woman's role in rape and sexual assault?

4. How have the Woman Rules impacted your understanding of rape and sexual assault and how has that impacted your parenting style?

Subgroup Discussion: Bodily Autonomy

1. Do you know someone who has experienced any of the violations of body autonomy discussed today (sexual assault, rape, rape-related pregnancy, reproductive coercion, abortion/coercion in abortion)? What do you think that was like for her?

2. Have you experienced any of the violations of body autonomy discussed today? What was that like for you?

3. If you know someone who shared that they have experienced a violation of body autonomy, how did you respond? How did the Woman Rules impact your response?

4. If you experienced the violation yourself, how did the experience impact your decision to become a mother? What was that like for you?

The following creative activity is an opportunity to express the consequences you have experienced due to living in a society where sexual violence, rape, and lack of bodily autonomy are commonplace. This activity offers an opportunity for you to be vulnerable and honest about your experiences to begin the healing process.

You are invited to draw a picture of yourself and focus on the ways that a lack of bodily autonomy and/or violations or your bodily autonomy have impacted you. You can focus on physical consequences if you have experienced a physical violation. You can also focus on the psychological, spiritual, and emotional consequences of any of the above topics discussed today.

Many women feel disconnected from themselves and may depict themselves as fragmented. Some women may depict themselves as blocked or guarded as the way they care for themselves. Some moms may struggle with physical affection, even with their own children as a result. For some moms, they may see themselves as chronically on the lookout for something bad to happen, both for themselves and their children, like a sheriff on patrol. Some may have adjusted their outside appearance in an attempt to push others away or create a sense of control. Like other art, the drawing you are invited to create uses visual imagery as an opportunity to express what may not always be easy for you to express in words. The hope is that by acknowledging the consequences, you can reclaim your autonomy and explore what aspects of these depictions you want to keep and what aspects of these depictions you may want to adjust or let go of completely.

You are reminded that this is not about the quality of the drawing itself, but rather the process of creating the art. We encourage you not to overthink your work and simply trust your intuition and your gut. If you focus on honesty with yourself, then no matter what you create, it will be meaningful.

Creative Activity: Reclaiming My Bodily Autonomy

Into Action: Engaging with My Body

Part 1: Please take some time to answer the following prompts as an opportunity to engage with your physical body differently. Think of the amazing things your body allows you to do. Examples could include activities like riding a bike, running, swimming, or grounded activities like deep breathing, feeling the earth beneath your feet, etc. Think of the ways your body cares for you like slowing down so you can sleep or speeding up to alert you when needed. Connect this to your healing journey for the ways your body cares for itself. Feel free to write your answers down first. If you're willing, the goal is to take your answers and read them or say them aloud to yourself. This is an opportunity to shift your relationship with your body and express gratitude toward it for all it has done and continues to do for you.

Thank you, body, for the way you allow me to _____.

Thank you, body, for protecting me by _____.

Thank you, body, for helping me heal by _____.

Part 2: If you have experienced an assault or a violation of your body and specific parts of your body carry your pain, we encourage you to focus on them and honor them as part of your healing. You can write down some ways to do that below:

Summary

Now that you have finished this meeting, we invite you to take a deep breath... and exhale. Well done! We know this was probably a difficult meeting to experience, but part of what the *Amazing Moms!* program is about is tackling the difficult topics to help you unlock the best of yourself.

You spent time in this meeting going through some of the violations of bodily autonomy that women and moms experience, learned about the idea of Rape Culture, and took a hard look at how the Woman Rules and Man Rules influence these phenomena. Part of the Toxic Water is the understanding that finding a sense of safety as a woman is inherently difficult. However, the creative activity was designed to help you take charge of reclaiming your own bodily autonomy through honesty and vulnerability with yourself. There is power in "calling out" the difficulties, traumas, and violations you have experienced. Once they are no longer lurking in the shadows, you can begin to address them head-on and remove their power over you.

That can look different for different moms. Some may be able to address their experiences on their own. Many others, though, will benefit by accessing additional support through things like counseling. There is no "right" way to continue healing yourself, but it is important you know that you do not have to take that journey solely on your own. Remind yourself that your own healing journey will have a positive impact on your children.

Moms and Trauma: Breaking the Cycle

This meeting focuses on a challenging topic, but one that is critical to explore as a mother. Trauma is a topic that is being discussed more openly, and with the increase in research and knowledge over recent decades we are learning how important it is to understand what trauma is, how it shows up differently for different people (e.g. women versus men), and how critical it is to make sure to get help if you have any history of trauma.

This meeting is not meant to replace trauma-related treatment such as therapy or medication. It is important to understand that this is meant as an educational opportunity to explore what trauma is and to give you more insight into what trauma looks like for women and mothers.

As you go through this meeting, recognize what comes up for you. This can easily be a triggering discussion about a very serious topic. Therefore, checking in with yourself as you learn the information and go through the activities is important. You are learning different skills and tools to be able to care for yourself at any given moment, so remember that you have those skills to access anytime you begin to feel angry, upset, frightened, or uncomfortable. Remember, you can reach out to someone else for help or support as well.

Amazing Moms! Motherhood Curriculum, Workbook, First Edition. Sophia Murphy, Dan Griffin, and Harrison Crawford.
© 2026 Sophia Murphy, Dan Griffin, and Harrison Crawford. Published 2026 by John Wiley & Sons, Inc.

The goals for Meeting 5 are:

1. To define trauma and learn how it can come from many different sources.
2. To become more aware of how trauma in mothers is impacted by the Woman Rules.
3. To recognize how common trauma is and that it does not reflect upon you as a woman.

Important Definition: Traumagenesis[1]

"Trauma is anything that pushes us past our ability to cope."

Important Concept: Window of Tolerance

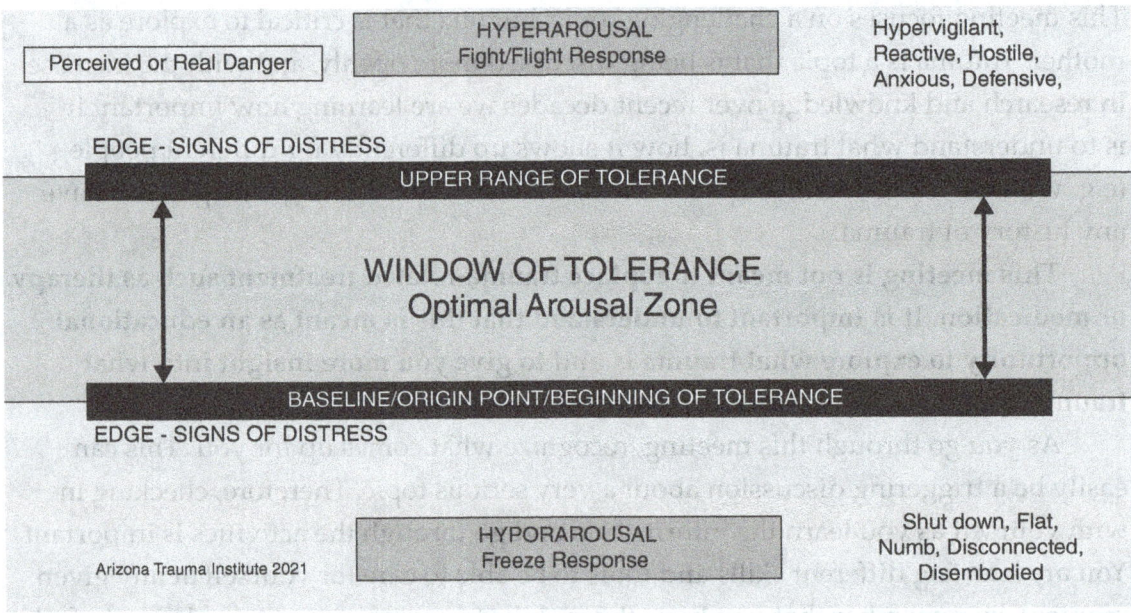

Source: Retrieved from: (Fletcher, 2022).

The Window of Tolerance was created by Dan Siegel, MD and offers a way to conceptualize and visualize the ideal range for managing stress. Dr. Siegel argued that for humans, there is a "window" where our nervous system functions at its best.

---

[1] Rhoton, R. and Aubrey, T.E.R. (2019). Transformative care a trauma focused. Transformative care: a trauma-focused approach to caregiving.

Anything above this window or below this window is considered below optimal. This is where we get the terms *hyper*arousal (pushed above the window) and *hypo*arousal (pushed below the window).

Hyperarousal is consistent with being "keyed up" which can include anxiety, racing thoughts, increased distractibility, anger, insomnia, and other experiences associated with excess energy. Hypoarousal is more consistent with low energy which includes depression, difficulty engaging in activities, poor concentration, low motivation, excessive sleepiness, and other experiences associated with lethargy.

Examples of Events That Could Result in Trauma (Black, 2018)

The following are examples of events that can result in trauma for an individual. These lists come from the book *Unspoken Legacy* by Dr. Claudia Black, and are not meant to be comprehensive. Also, please remember that everybody experiences events differently, so not all the examples listed are experienced as traumatic by every person.

Big-T Traumas may be responses to:

- War, invasion, attack, violent revolution, an act of terrorism, etc.
- Natural disasters such as floods, fires, hurricanes, landslides, etc.
- Rape
- Sexual or physical abuse
- Violence in the home
- Car, train, plane, or bus accidents
- Crime victimization
- Captivity
- Serious injury or illness
- Acts of racism
- Witnessing violence
- Chronic neglect, especially among children and the elderly
- The unexpected death of someone close to you
- Forced relocation, becoming a refugee, living in an internment camp, etc.

Small-t traumas may be responses to:

- Failing at something important to you
- Losses (the loss of a friend, a prized possession, a hoped-for promotion, etc.)
- High stress at work or school
- Harsh, unfair, or extreme criticism
- Rejection
- Being bullied
- Being shamed or demeaned
- Being yelled at
- Being ignored, disrespected, or discounted
- Betrayal
- Control or manipulation by someone you trust, especially an authority figure
- Discovering or witnessing the infidelity of your partner or parent
- Inconsistent or contradictory responses from a parent or partner
- A lack of empathy from a parent or partner
- Unrealistic expectations
- An acrimonious divorce
- Spiritual boundary violations (e.g. if someone uses his or her religious authority to control you or if you're sent for extensive training in a religion you don't believe in)
- Enmeshment (not being allowed to have your own thoughts, feelings, and desires)

Moms and Trauma: The Role of Attachment

Attachment is something incredibly important and it is impacted by trauma. When infants are born, they have an innate need to attach to others because connection is at the heart of the human experience. What's important to know is that you attach to whatever is present in your life, whether it is healthy for you or not. Your caregiver(s) may not have been able to be there for you the way you needed them to be – as loving and supportive people, yet you formed an attachment to them because as an infant you didn't know better, or there may have been no other options. This experience can result in different types of dysfunctional attachment styles. If you were lucky enough to have had a relatively healthy upbringing, you're likely to have a secure attachment style and are usually able to navigate intimacy knowing how to balance independence with interdependence.

Depending on how unhealthy your early caregivers were, your attachment to them can set the stage for childhood trauma. If your caregivers were unwilling or unable to give you safety, comfort, support, and love, the likelihood of experiencing trauma in some form was increased. Attachment plays an important role in our experience with trauma and relationships.

It is important to recognize two distinct types of traumas that have been identified: intergenerational trauma and historical trauma.

Important Definition: Intergenerational Trauma

"Transmission of trauma between generations of a family. People who experienced adverse childhood experiences growing up, or who survived historical disasters or traumas, may pass the effects of those traumas on to their children or grandchildren, through their genes, their behavior, or both, leaving the next generation susceptible to anxiety, depression, hypervigilance, and other emotional and mental health concerns."

– Psychology Today www.psychologytoday.com/us/basics/
intergenerational-trauma

Important Definition: Historical Trauma

"Historical trauma is multigenerational trauma experienced by a specific cultural, racial or ethnic group. It is related to major events that oppressed a particular group of people because of their status as oppressed, such as slavery, the Holocaust, forced migration, and the violent colonization of Native Americans."

– Administration for Children and Families (ACF)
www.acf.hhs.gov/trauma-toolkit/trauma-concept

It is important to recognize that trauma can come from past generations as well as being part of one or more groups that experienced trauma in the past. Intergenerational trauma refers to the way in which trauma can be passed down through generations, usually in families. An example of this could be children who were in foster care and abused, who then grew up and had difficulty with attachment to their own children. The parents' traumatic experience impacted their children's, passing trauma down through the family generations.

Historical trauma refers to whole groups of people who have experienced trauma and the lasting effects of those experiences continue to impact members of those groups today. Common examples of historical trauma include the Holocaust and slavery, and the impact those events had on the groups of people who suffered, but also how that impact still shows in those groups today for members who did not directly experience those events. And those are just a couple of examples of some very deep wounds that exist in communities around the world and greatly affect the generations of individuals living there.

The activity that comes next is meant to take whatever form works best for you. This is an opportunity to think about and express your life experiences in a creative way, without having to write anything and without any specific requirements for how to complete it. You are invited to consider your life in different periods of time (e.g. childhood, adolescence, young adulthood, and adulthood) and create a representation of your experiences during those times that are meaningful for you. You are encouraged to use colors, images, and drawings, but go with your instinct on what will be best for you.

You will notice that the Into Action exercise that follows this meeting asks you to add to this artistic project in a unique way. Take your time on this and simply focus on making it meaningful to you.

Creative Activity: The Colors of Life

Five Senses Mindfulness Exercise

This exercise is a simple and effective way to practice being in the present moment, in the "here and now." Find a quiet place where you can practice this for about 5–10 minutes without interruption. As you go through the steps, take about 15–30 seconds in between to give yourself time to experience each sense.

1. *Hearing*: Spend a few moments focusing on what you hear. Notice the different sounds, perhaps ones you didn't hear initially. Suspend any judgment of them. They are neither good nor bad, they just are.
2. *Smell*: Shift your attention to any smells you pick up. Again, notice them without assigning any judgment of good or bad, just that they are.
3. *Touch*: Focus on your sense of touch. Notice the feeling of the fabric of your clothes, or wherever your hands are resting. Notice the sensation of sitting in the chair, your feet on the ground.
4. *Sight*: Concentrate on your sense of sight by just observing what is around you. There are many things you could notice, from the different shades of color to different textures of the objects around you. Avoid judging the sights, and just observe them and then move to the next one.
5. *Taste*: Shift your attention to your sense of taste. If you have a snack, feel free to take a small bite. If not, notice any taste inside your mouth now, or the taste of the air you're breathing, again suspending judgment.

The activity you are invited to complete before the next meeting uses the Colors of Life activity you started during the meeting and adds a component of resilience and healing. Read on for how you can make this activity even more meaningful.

Into Action: Kintsugi

Thinking about trauma and how it affects you can be a difficult idea to face. Moms often experience guilt or shame about past experiences that may have been traumatic. Many times, the Woman Rules play into those feelings of guilt and shame, telling women and moms that to acknowledge trauma is selfish and overdramatic, or that somehow they are to blame for what happened to them. Many women struggle to acknowledge trauma because of the messages they've received to always be perfect. We challenged that in this meeting.

There is a Japanese art form called Kintsugi, where broken pottery is fixed using precious metal lacquer to mend the broken pieces together. This art does not try to hide blemishes and previous breaks but instead highlights them in a more beautiful way. The broken object does not hide from its history but acknowledges it and understands that history, however fractured, is a part of itself.

You can begin shifting how you view your past experiences. You can hide from them and bury them deep inside. Or you can recognize them as part of your history and work to mend yourself in ways that will help you be brighter and more valuable than before.

With this in mind, your Into Action practice is to look over your Colors of Life project from this meeting. Identify where there may have been cracks in need of mending, or seams coming undone. Perhaps these relate to the more difficult times in your life, and where those fall on your paper. Next, fill those cracks or seams with positivity and hope. Perhaps for you, that means drawing over the seams in your favorite color or using gold or silver colors to represent the value that can be added to your life through the process of beginning to heal. Or choose a different method to mend those cracks and seams that will still highlight the value and importance of doing so. You may have only one crack or seam to fix, or you might have many. Giving time and care to mending them is important for your journey as a conscious mother.

You will not be asked to share this project with anyone, though you may choose to do so if you feel ready to share it with a trusted friend or partner. Be aware of what feelings come up for you when completing this project, including in the days after completing it. Practice some of the grounding and relaxation skills you have started learning in this program.

Practical & Tactical – Trauma Signs Self-Reflection

The following are some questions related to signs of trauma. Answer each question by circling the number, 1–5, that fits best for you:

• How often do you say "yes" to requests when you rather say "no" out of concerns for how the other person will see you?

1-Never 2-Rarely 3-Sometimes 4-Often 5-Always

• How often do you yell at other people and/or your children or put them down in hurtful ways?

     1-Never 2-Rarely 3-Sometimes 4-Often 5-Always

• How often do you mock your partner and/or children or become uncomfortable when he or she cries or expresses vulnerability?

     1-Never 2-Rarely 3-Sometimes 4-Often 5-Always

• How often do you find yourself criticizing yourself for not doing enough or thinking you should do more?

     1-Never 2-Rarely 3-Sometimes 4-Often 5-Always

• When you feel close to someone, how often do you find yourself hyperfocusing on them, worrying about what they think of you, or trying to "be" who you think they want you to be?

     1-Never 2-Rarely 3-Sometimes 4-Often 5-Always

• How often do you suppress difficult emotions like anger or sadness in front of your children or partner out of concern for making them feel bad?

     1-Never 2-Rarely 3-Sometimes 4-Often 5-Always

• When you feel sad or hurt, how often do you turn to tasks or keeping yourself busy?

     1-Never 2-Rarely 3-Sometimes 4-Often 5-Always

• How often do you feel resentful and expect others to just know what you need at any given time?

     1-Never 2-Rarely 3-Sometimes 4-Often 5-Always

• How easily startled are you?

     1-Never 2-Rarely 3-Sometimes 4-Often 5-Always

• How easy is it for you to ask for help?

     1-Never 2-Rarely 3-Sometimes 4-Often 5-Always

• How easy is it for you to accept help when offered?

     1-Never 2-Rarely 3-Sometimes 4-Often 5-Always

• How often do you have nightmares of past experiences from your life?

     1-Never 2-Rarely 3-Sometimes 4-Often 5-Always

Does any of this sound familiar to you? If so, it is just information, not a scientific assessment or diagnosis. However, it probably means it would be useful to have a conversation with a professional who understands trauma. You are not crazy, or a bad person. But you may need help to heal. Give yourself, and your loved ones, that gift.

Summary

While this may have been a difficult meeting for you, the hope is that you now have a better understanding of what trauma is and how it shows up for women and moms. You learned how the Woman Rules are often imposed on girls in traumatic ways, and then the Woman Rules stop girls and women from wanting to seek help or support for what they are going through. Trauma is very complicated, unique to each person, and something that we still need to understand better.

Remember that you have multiple tools available to you to cope with any strong feelings or reactions to this meeting. This workbook contains all the different breathing, grounding, and relaxation exercises from the program, so use this as a resource to help you with any challenging reactions you have. You also have support available to you from your meeting facilitator(s), so reach out to her/him/them if you experience any difficulties, strong feelings, or confusion after this meeting.

As someone committed to being a conscious mother, you can explore your own history and experiences and decide the best ways for you to heal. Remember: we repeat what we don't repair. You have a unique opportunity now to repair any hurt from your past, and this will help you to become the most amazing mom you can be.

MEETING 6

Making the Connections – Mental Health, Addiction, and Trauma

This meeting continues the theme of connecting our history and experiences to our current reality. In this meeting, you will learn about the ways in which past challenging experiences still can impact you throughout your life. It is important to keep in mind, though, that this is simply information and not something designed to frighten you or increase your stress. When approaching this subject, you might find it helpful to consider how to use this information to increase your awareness of the past's influence on you now, as well as think about ways to seek support for anything you may struggle with, now or in the future.

The goals of Meeting 6 are:

1. To explore the overlap of mental health challenges, addiction, and trauma through looking at the Adverse Childhood Experiences study.
2. To develop self-awareness of your needs in these areas, if any, and explore how to begin making positive changes.
3. To develop awareness of what needs your children might experience so you are prepared.

Amazing Moms! Motherhood Curriculum, Workbook, First Edition. Sophia Murphy, Dan Griffin, and Harrison Crawford.
© 2026 Sophia Murphy, Dan Griffin, and Harrison Crawford. Published 2026 by John Wiley & Sons, Inc.

4. To explore your own resilience and ability to seek support to get your needs addressed to help you become the best mother you can be.

Advanced Box Breathing

In this meeting, you begin practicing Advanced Box Breathing involves breathing in, holding, breathing out, and resting for six seconds versus four like you were doing previously. This can help deepen the relaxation that comes with the breathing exercise. The description of this exercise is below for your reference:

1. Take a couple of normal breaths. Try moving your breath deeper into your lower abdomen so you're not breathing shallowly in your chest.
2. Take a breath slowly through your nose, counting to six. One, two, three, four, five, six.
3. Hold your breath for a count of six. One, two, three, four, five, six.
4. Slowly exhale out your mouth as you count to six one more time. One, two, three, four, five, six.
5. Rest for six more counts before you start again. One, two, three, four, five, six.
6. Try it again.
7. As thoughts come up, acknowledge them and then return your focus to your breathing and counting.
8. Go through two more rounds of this advanced box breathing on your own, counting to yourself.

The next exercise will probably be one you have not experienced before. It combines deep breathing with alternating tapping, which research has shown to help decrease feelings of anxiety and stress. It may feel strange at first, but give it time and practice and it might just become your favorite exercise!

Eagle's Wings

1. Take a few deep breaths from down in your abdomen.
2. Next, cross your hands across your chest so the tips of your middle fingers are just below your collarbone. The rest of your fingers will lay relaxed on your upper chest.

3. Try to have your fingers pointing up instead of outward. You can interlock your thumbs if this helps make it easier.

4. Now, slowly and steadily alternate tapping your hands on your chest repeatedly: right, left, right, left, resembling the flapping wings of an eagle.

5. Continue to take slow, deep breaths and continue tapping steadily.

6. Notice what is going through your mind and body: whether it be thoughts, images, feelings, or physical sensations.

7. Notice these things coming and going as you would watch clouds passing in the sky.

8. Continue breathing slowly and deeply.

9. Continue tapping: right, left, right, left, right, left.

10. When you feel in your body that you are relaxed, grounded, and it has been enough, you may stop.

If you want to know more about tapping and the positive effects it can have, a simple Internet search will give you information. If you search for "bilateral stimulation," you will find information that describes the science behind this exercise.

Adverse Childhood Experiences (ACEs)

The Adverse Childhood Experiences study, also known as the ACE study asked thousands of people to answer questions about experiences they may have had in childhood and adolescence, specifically negative experiences. Questions ranged from whether participants witnessed abuse in the home, experienced divorce growing up, were abused themselves, or were not able to have their needs met.

The researchers were able to make connections between the adverse childhood experiences of the participants and many other difficulties the participants experienced later in life. There was a connection between having experienced traumatic events in childhood and outcomes later in life like being diagnosed with a mental health condition, developing an addictive disorder, having physical health issues such as obesity and heart disease, and so many more. This study was an incredibly important moment in our understanding of how our minds and bodies are connected, and the impact that childhood trauma has on the mind and the body in ways we didn't understand before this study.

How does this relate to you as a mother? First, this information may give you some insight into some of your own experiences, both growing up and as a mother now. Perhaps you experienced some of the challenges that this study points to as being connected to adverse childhood experiences. Secondly, you can use this information as part of your work to become the best mother you can. Remember: we repeat what we don't repair. As a mom who is committed to becoming the best you can be, hopefully you recognize some of what you may have experienced growing up and make conscious, intentional decisions to prevent the repetition of those experiences for your own children.

Please fill out the ACE study below. Remember, this is just about collecting information about your experiences to help inform how you take care of yourself from now on. As you answer the questions, go with your first instinct, and do your best not to overthink how to answer.

While you were growing up, during your first 18 years of life:

Did a parent or other adult in the household often or very often: YES or NO
Swear at you, insult you, put you down, or humiliate you OR act in a
way that made you afraid that you might be physically hurt?

Did a parent or other adult in the household often or very often: YES or NO
Push, grab, slap, or throw something at you OR hit you so hard that
you had marks or were injured?

Did an adult or person at least 5 years older than you ever: Touch or   YES or NO
fondle you or have you touch their body in a sexual way OR attempt
or actually have oral, anal, or vaginal intercourse with you?

Did you often or very often feel that: No one in your family loved you   YES or NO
or thought you were important or special OR your family didn't look
out for each other, feel close to each other, or support each other?

Did you often or very often feel that: You didn't have enough to eat,   YES or NO
had to wear dirty clothes, and had no one to protect you OR your
parents were too drunk or high to take care of you or take you to the
doctor if you needed it?

Was your mother or stepmother or father or stepfather: Often or very   YES or NO
often pushed, grabbed, slapped, or had something thrown at her/him
OR sometimes, often, or very often kicked, bitten, hit with a fist, or hit
with something hard OR ever repeatedly hit for at least a few minutes
or threatened with a knife or gun?

Were your parents ever separated or divorced?   YES or NO

Did you live with anyone who was a problem-drinker or alcoholic or   YES or NO
who used street drugs or prescription drugs not as prescribed?

Was a household member depressed or mentally ill or did a   YES or NO
household member attempt suicide?

Did a household member go to prison?   YES or NO

ACE Score (total of all "YES" answers): _____.

Important Definition: Mental Health

"Mental health is our emotional, psychological, and social well-being. It affects how
we think, feel, and act, and helps determine how we handle stress, relate to others,
and make choices."

> – Substance Abuse and Mental Health Services Administration definition
> www.samhsa.gov/Mental-health

Important Definition: Addiction

"A treatable, chronic medical disease involving complex interactions among brain
circuits, genetics, the environment, and an individual's life experiences. People with
addiction use substances or engage in behaviors that become compulsive and often
continue despite harmful consequences."

> – American Society of Addiction Medicine definition www.asam.org/
> quality-care/definition-of-addiction

Subgroup Discussion: Let's Get Real

Next, you have an opportunity to explore your own mental health and addiction
needs in your small group. This is not an activity designed to create shame or
judgment. Much of what is done in this program is meant to simply give you
awareness and get you thinking about these topics in ways you might not have before.
Keep that in mind as you answer the following questions.

1. On a scale of 1 to 10, one being no concern at all, what is your level of concern for your own mental health? Why did you choose that rating?

2. On a scale of 1 to 10, how concerned do you think your *loved ones* are about your mental health? Why did you choose that rating?

3. On a scale of 1 to 10, what is your level of concern about potential addiction issues you may be experiencing? Why did you choose that rating?

4. On a scale of 1 to 10, how concerned do you think your *loved ones* are about potential addiction issues on your part? Why did you choose that rating?

5. What fears or concerns do you have about acknowledging and/or discussing these topics?

Important Definition: Resilience

"Resilience is the process and outcome of successfully adapting to difficult or challenging life experiences, especially through mental, emotional, and behavioral flexibility and adjustment to external and internal demands."
– American Psychological Association definition
https://www.apa.org/topics/resilience

Next is a new grounding and breathing exercise for you to practice and use. Practicing gratitude is shown to have real benefits for your mental health and any recovery you are working on in your life. Adding gratitude practice to some simple breathing creates a strong combination in one brief exercise.

Exercise: Gratitude Breathing

Take a minute or two to identify three things you are grateful for in this moment. They do not need to be "huge" things. Even the small things are worth your gratitude. Write these three items down here:

1.

2.

3.

Next, make yourself comfortable and prepare to do some deep breathing:

- Take a deep breath in through your nose, pause, and exhale fully through your mouth.
- Repeat this again.
- Now, with each full breath you take in through your nose, pause, and say one of your gratitude items to yourself either out loud or in your mind.
- After you state your gratitude, exhale your breath fully through your mouth.
- Take another full breath through your nose, but this time as you pause with your full breath in, say another one of your gratitude items to yourself.
- Exhale the full breath through your mouth.
- Repeat this a third time, saying your third gratitude item to yourself before you exhale fully.
- Take a couple of minutes to repeat this same process until you have repeated each of your gratitude items three times.

As you finish this breathing exercise, slowly return to the here and now.

Practicing gratitude can help build resilience. Even thinking about small things you are grateful for helps strengthen your "resilience muscles." Writing them down adds another layer to the positive effect that this can have.

This can also be turned into a cool activity to practice with your children. Have them practice gratitude – getting them to develop this habit now can have a big payoff throughout their lives!

This meeting may have challenged you, but the hope is that you recognize the importance of knowing how your experiences impact you (or might impact you in the future). Hopefully, you also learned that you are fully capable of building resilience in yourself, as well as helping your children build resilience. The activity you're invited to complete before the next meeting involves thinking about the ways you can practice and build resilience. Consider involving your children in these activities as well to help them build good habits of their own.

Into Action: Resilience-Building Plan

As discussed in the meeting, resilience is a skill you can build just like working out a muscle. The more you use it and practice it, the more resilient you can become. You will find multiple recommendations for how to practice resilience and continue building your resilience capacity. For this Into Action activity, you are encouraged to complete one section per day over the next week. You do not have to go in order but spending a few minutes each day will help you work on all the following areas to build resilience in a manageable way.

Recognize Your Signs of Stress

- Where do you feel stress in your body? (e.g. headaches, tense muscles in your neck, tightness in your chest, and/or stomach aches)

- What are some of the unhealthy habits you engage in when feeling stressed? (e.g. overeating, using alcohol or other drugs, and/or not exercising)

- What are some of the positive habits you engage in when feeling stressed (e.g. exercise, organizing your time, and/or seeking support from others)?

Focus on Building Physical Hardiness

- What kind of small changes can you invest in to improve your health? (e.g. better sleep, better nutrition, hydration, exercise, etc.)

- List one small change you can make now:

Strengthen the Relaxation Response – Calm Body and Calm Mind

- List some activities at home that could help you relax (Tip: there are many listed in the appendix of this workbook if you want ideas).

- List some activities at work that could help you relax (Tip: there are many listed in the appendix of this workbook if you want ideas).

- Try out some new relaxation skills such as mindfulness or meditation apps such as Calm or Headspace (not promoting these specifically, just offered as examples).

- Try some self-soothing activities such as:
  - Tactile (holding something comforting or soothing)
  - Smell (smell of lavender, fresh air)
  - Visual (puppy or kitten photos, looking out the window, etc.)
  - Auditory (listen to music, listen to sounds of nature)
  - Taste (drinking some tea, eating chocolate)

Identify and Use Your Strengths

- Describe a time when you were able to overcome or handle a major challenge in life.

- What did you learn about yourself?

- What personal strengths did you use?

- How might you apply these strengths now?

Increase Positive Emotions on a Daily Basis

- Identify sources of humor or joy.

- Express gratitude, visit someone, or write a letter.

- List your accomplishments.

Engage in Meaningful Activities

- Notice what happened in your day that was meaningful on a regular basis.

- What kinds of activities did you find meaningful?

- Identify activities that put you in the flow (enjoyable things you do that cause you to lose track of time). List some of them below.

Counter Unhelpful Thinking

- Write down what you are thinking about when you get stressed and then ask the following:
  - What is the worst that can happen, and could I survive it?

  - What is the best thing that could happen?

  - What would I tell a friend in a similar situation?

  - If you can't stop thinking about something, write about it a couple of times over a 4-week period for about 15 minutes each time. Notice how your story changes or your perspective becomes clearer each time.

  - Remember a hero, a coach, or a mentor who encouraged you when you doubted yourself. Write about your experience with this person.

Create a Caring Community

- Surround yourself with positive and healthy people. Connect with friends and family on a regular basis (e.g. via phone, FaceTime, Zoom, and especially in person).

- When can you connect with them next? Put dates and times down below and try to stick to it.

- Identify your sources of support, at work, at home, and in the community. Who are your supports? List some of them here and keep adding to the list over time.

- Practice good communication and conflict resolution skills (more to come on these in the *Amazing Moms!* program).

Adapted from: https://positivepsychology.com/resilience-activities-exercises/#science-based-activities

Practical & Tactical: Complete the PACEs Questionnaire

Having answered the ACEs questionnaire in the meeting, we encourage you to take some time to answer a similar questionnaire, but one that has a very important difference: The questionnaire is called the Protective and Compensatory Experiences (PACE) questionnaire because the questions ask about protective factors and positive events from your childhood.

When you were growing up, before your 18th birthday:

Did you have someone who loved you unconditionally (you did not doubt that they cared about you)?   YES or NO

Did you have at least one best friend (someone you could trust, had fun with)?   YES or NO

Did you do anything regularly to help others (e.g., volunteer   YES or NO
at a hospital, nursing home, church) or do special projects
in the community to help others (food drives, Habitat for
Humanity)?

Were you regularly involved in organized sports groups   YES or NO
(e.g., soccer, basketball, track) or other physical activity
(e.g., competitive cheer, gymnastics, dance, marching band)?

Were you an active member of at least one civic group or   YES or NO
a non-sport social group such as scouts, church, or youth
group?

Did you have an engaging hobby – an artistic or intellectual   YES or NO
pastime either alone or in a group (e.g., chess club, debate
team, musical instrument or vocal group, theater, spelling bee,
or did you read a lot)?

Was there an adult (not your parent) you trusted and could   YES or NO
count on when you needed help or advice (e.g., coach, teacher,
minister, neighbor, relative)?

Was your home typically clean AND safe with enough   YES or NO
food to eat?

Overall, did your schools provide the resources and academic   YES or NO
experiences you needed to learn?

In your home, were there rules that were clear and fairly   YES or NO
administered?

PACE Score (total of all "YES" answers): _____

Summary

There are clear connections between adverse childhood experiences (ACEs), recent adverse experiences (something the ACE study did not include), and current or future mental health challenges and/or challenges with addiction. After this meeting, you should have a better sense of how these things connect as well as a better understanding of your own experiences and how they may impact you today or in the future.

Negativity, shame, and judgment are major factors in the reluctance women and moms have about admitting to and seeking help for their mental health needs. The stigma is equally bad (or worse) for individuals experiencing addiction. The problem is that the more we ignore it, the more it grows and causes problems on an individual level and in society as a whole. This meeting was designed to help you better understand how addiction, mental health, and trauma are connected and how being intentional about seeking support for any or all of those areas can have massive positive results for you and your children.

It's not all doom and gloom, though. This meeting also highlighted the idea of resilience and how you can build resilience for yourself and for your children. Resilience is another skill you can develop and use to offset the challenges you face in life. Part of being a conscious mother is recognizing where you can direct your focus and energy that will have the most positive impact, and resilience-building is a worthy cause. As you think about what was discussed in this meeting, recognize that you are now armed with more information and the ability to use it for your benefit and for the benefit of your children.

Feelings... Nothing More Than Feelings

Meeting 7 begins an in-depth discussion about how mothers experience, deal with, and understand their own emotions, and how that translates to their *parenting*. We explore the emotion of shame and begin to understand how the Woman Rules often result in placing unrealistic expectations on ourselves, which leads to shame when we struggle to meet those unrealistic expectations. You will learn a new tool called Digging Deeper, which will help you to be more real in your relationships, especially with your children. You will get the opportunity to look at mistakes you may have made with your children and how to do those same interactions differently with new tools of emotional awareness.

The goals of Meeting 7 are:

1. To take a deeper look at emotions and the relationship mothers have with them.
2. To learn about shame and why it is the most common emotion associated with women and mothers.
3. To learn skills that can help you regulate your emotions and respond to them effectively.
4. To build skills that can help you teach your children about emotions and how to respond to their own feelings.

Amazing Moms! Motherhood Curriculum, Workbook, First Edition. Sophia Murphy, Dan Griffin, and Harrison Crawford.
© 2026 Sophia Murphy, Dan Griffin, and Harrison Crawford. Published 2026 by John Wiley & Sons, Inc.

Important Definition: Guilt

"The feeling you experience as a cue that you have done something that steps outside of your values." Guilt is a focus on behavior – 'I did something bad'.

— Brene Brown in her Ted Talk, "Listening to shame"

Important Definitions: Shame

"The intensely painful feeling or experience of believing that we are flawed and therefore unworthy of love and belonging – something we've experienced, done, or failed to do makes us unworthy of connection."

— Brene Brown
brenebrown.com/articles/2013/01/15/shame-v-guilt/

"Shame is a focus on the self – 'I *am* bad'."

— Brene Brown in her Ted Talk, "Listening to shame"

Important Definition: Resentment

Resentment is the feeling we experience when we have pushed past our own boundaries or allowed someone else to push past our boundaries through inaction (passivity, overly agreeable).

Women and Feelings

We know that all girls and all women experience a whole range of emotions – fear, sadness, hurt, joy, shame, anger, and numerous others. However, as you explored when learning about the Woman Rules, women are restricted from experiencing any emotions seen as negative, which becomes exhausting and inauthentic. The emotions you experience are as diverse and intricate as each person is. Your feelings color your experiences and give them meaning. The problem is that when you ignore your feelings or become disconnected from them, you miss out on a significant part of your life. Your life is not nearly as vibrant as it could be.

The Woman Rules tell you to only show positive emotions in order to present as agreeable. So much attention and focus are aimed at being selfless.

Consider what you learned from the Woman Rules about feelings and what versions of yourself you're allowed to show. Now, think about your children.

What messages are you sending to them, intentionally or not, about feelings and how to "be?" What are the messages you *want* to send to them about feelings and how to show up? What are you saying versus what are you *doing?* Do you want your boys to learn that feelings should be bottled up, ignored, or only expressed through anger? Do you want your girls to focus on being "nice," on being agreeable and selfless to a fault? Do you want your children, regardless of gender, to believe that their trauma is just weakness, and sharing about and seeking help for their trauma is undesirable? Do you want your girls to learn that they can only express their feelings with other females and that they need to avoid anger because it's not appropriate or "ladylike?" The good news is that *you* get to choose to do something differently for yourself and your children, if you would like to. The path to doing things differently starts with awareness and becomes a habit through practice. This is what it means to be a conscious mother.

Prompts for Digging Deeper Activity

Think about the most recent time you were angry with your children. Write your responses to the following prompts about that situation:

1. Describe the situation (who was there, what led up to it, any other details):

2. How aware were you that you felt angry in that moment? If you weren't, when did you realize it after the fact?

3. How did your anger show up? Was it passive, passive-aggressive, or did you turn your anger inward and become self-critical, self-shaming, or was it externally projected or aggressive?

4. Once you noticed your anger, how did you physically feel? Where in your body did you notice any physical sensations?

5. How do you think shame may have contributed to your experience of anger (awareness or lack of)?

6. How did your expression of (or lack of expression of) shame/anger impact those around you?

7. How did you feel afterward?

8. How do you think being able to acknowledge your shame and anger and communicate it effectively may have improved the situation?

Optional Scenarios for Digging Deeper Activity

1. You have prompted your child three times to put his shoes on to be able to leave for school. Each time he has responded by saying, "Ok, I will," but he has not yet gotten his shoes on. You have to drop him off at school before heading to work, where you have an important meeting scheduled for right when you are supposed to be there. You are now running late. Describe what happens next using the prompts.

2. Your child has a habit of throwing things when she is upset. You have talked to her numerous times about how that is not appropriate behavior, but she continues to do it. Today you come home from a long day at work, and she asks you for ice cream. You tell her she has to wait until after dinner, and she immediately throws a book that is in her hands to the floor, breaking the cover off the book. She then starts to use a whining voice repeatedly saying, "I want ice cream now." Describe what happens next using the prompts.

3. You are putting your child's clothes into his drawers after doing laundry when you come across a bag of marijuana hidden in the drawer. You have made it clear before that there is no drug or alcohol use allowed. Just then, your child walks into the room. You ask him about the marijuana, and the response you get is, "At least I'm not shooting up meth." Describe what happens next using the prompts.

4. You are a single mom with a one-month-old baby. It is 3 a.m. and you have not gone to sleep yet because your baby is crying and crying for seemingly no reason. The baby is fed, has a clean diaper, and does not seem to be sick. You hold the baby, rock the baby, and try everything you can think of to soothe the baby, but nothing is working. The baby keeps crying and crying. Describe what happens next using the prompts…

This next activity gives you space to draw a scene that shows how anger might be helpful in your life. For example, you may draw a situation where your anger is trying to tell you something and listening to it would be beneficial. Please consider the positives of anger and explore how to listen to it as a valid, valuable emotion. Please remember it is not about the quality of the art, but about giving you a chance to put your experience down in a creative form.

Creative Activity: A Picture of Anger

This next guided imagery exercise can be truly amazing as you practice it. Allow yourself about five minutes of uninterrupted time to go through this, whether you record it and listen back to it or have someone read this aloud to you softly. Your workbook offers different versions of this exercise as you will see as you continue through the program. You are encouraged not to worry about "how well" you're doing the exercise or if you're doing it "right." We simply invite you to avoid judgment of yourself and go through the exercise as best you can.

Place of Peace Relaxation Exercise

1. Take a deep breath in while you silently count to four. One, two, three, four.
2. Now breathe out slowly, silently counting to four again. One, two, three, four.
3. Remember to breathe from your abdomen. Breathe in again. One, two, three, four.
4. And out again. One, two, three, four.
5. Now picture in your mind a place of peace. Maybe you have been there before or maybe it is a place of your dreams. Maybe it's your bed or a comfortable chair. Maybe it's sitting by a lake or lying in the sun by the ocean. Maybe it's a special place you visited as a child or a scene from one of your favorite movies. It may be a real place or an imaginary place. See that place in your mind.
6. Keep breathing slowly and deeply.
7. Let the muscles in your face relax.
8. Let your brow relax.
9. Let your jaw relax.
10. Let your neck and your shoulders relax.
11. Imagine all the tension draining out of them. Let it go.
12. Let your hands and arms go limp next to you.
13. Let your middle relax – your chest and your abdomen.
14. Keep breathing in and out.
15. Let your hips and your legs relax.
16. Let your feet relax.
17. Relax your whole body and imagine yourself in that favorite, safe place. This is your place of peace. You are safe in this place. Your life is the life you always wanted it to be. You are the loving and caring mother you want to be.
18. Your life is full of peace. You are full of peace.
19. As you breathe in these next couple of times, breathe in the word "Peace."

20. As you breathe out, exhale all the pain from your past and all the negative feelings and thoughts.

21. Breathe in peace.

22. Breathe out pain.

Repeat the breathing process several more times.

Into Action

Shame is a difficult emotion to identify and process for many people. Today we discussed the importance of differentiating guilt from shame. Think of a recent time when you had an interaction and felt "bad" for something but couldn't quite identify where that feeling was coming from. You're invited to reflect on what was happening and answer the following questions to see if you can differentiate any feelings of guilt from feelings of shame:

1. Was the "bad" feeling related to something specific you wish you had done differently? Or was it related to the situation more generally, for example, seeing your child upset or seeing your partner upset? Or was it a combination of both?

2. If you identified that the bad feeling was due to a behavior, what was something you could have done differently? Try to choose a specific behavior or action.

3. If you couldn't identify a specific behavior you could have changed, then it is likely that the "bad" feeling was shame. Think of any negative or critical thoughts you had about yourself and list them below.

4. Shame often comes from messages we have internalized, usually related to unrealistic expectations. What was a message you received growing up about expectations that likely contributed to feeling shame in the scenario you have been remembering?

5. What is a more compassionate message you could give yourself now?

Practical & Tactical

Shame thrives on secrecy, silence, and judgment. When we keep our pain to ourselves, we reinforce the idea that we are flawed or broken. Pick one person in your life who you can have a conversation about shame with and explore how it impacts you as a woman and a mother. With this other person, discuss how shame also impacts your ability to feel angry and how feeling anger may improve your life. Write your reflections below:

Summary

Developing comfort with exploring your feelings and emotions in an honest way is a big part of becoming a healthy, conscious mother. Women and mothers are so often focused on how they will be perceived that they experience tremendous pressure to always appear "perfect." This hyperfocus on how they are perceived makes it incredibly difficult to have self-awareness and allow themselves to feel emotions freely, let alone express them vulnerably. Because of the Woman Rules, mothers often become trapped in the "Don'ts" and "Bes," and put their attention on everyone else at their own expense.

The unrealistic expectations created by the Rules keep women and mothers stuck. Women often experience intense shame when they can't be perfect because they believe perfection is the goal. However, in this program, you have been encouraged to recognize that perfection is a myth. Moving away from perfection creates space to feel *all* emotions and be a person with wants and needs. While denying difficult emotions like shame and anger might seem helpful, denial prevents you from being authentic. Mothers may look selfless when they never express a need or never express anger, but that is not their reality. All people experience anger and deserve to share it safely. The inability to do this negatively impacts our experiences as humans. This severe limitation of emotions will only cause problems in your relationships with your children and others. Healthy relationships require vulnerability, sharing of feelings, and the ability to repair hurt feelings. Raising children requires you to manage all sorts of difficult, changing, and confusing emotions for this little human who doesn't know how to manage them himself or herself.

This meeting challenged you to recognize your patterns in interpreting your emotional experience. Understanding shame is a great way to understand what so many moms do with uncomfortable emotions: deny them. It's also a great start to exploring your anger and better understanding the costs of ignoring it. Allowing yourself to feel and express anger, in healthy ways, allows you to be more authentic with yourself and others.

As someone committed to conscious motherhood, you have started to learn the tools for understanding your emotional life which will translate into being better able to help your children do the same. You get to be the example for them, so embracing growth in your emotional intelligence will have positive impacts on your children no matter what.

Exploring Family Dynamics, Past and Present

In this meeting, we first explore the Man Rules, the other half of the Rules of Gender. While not everyone subscribes to the Rules of Gender, most individuals do (often without thinking about it), and it is important for women to understand what men must live with and how they are expected to act and feel. Then we look at the impact your family of origin had on your life and your subsequent experiences as a woman and a mother. You will learn four common roles in families – hero, invisible child, scapegoat, and mascot – and begin to look at how the role you played in your family growing up has followed you into adulthood and may even be impacting how you show up as a mother.

The goals of Meeting 8 are:

1. To learn some common patterns in family relationships and recognize how those patterns may show up in your current family.
2. To discover how your family of origin was influenced by the Woman Rules and the Man Rules, and passed the Rules down.
3. To use your creativity to develop a Family of Origin Project.

Amazing Moms! Motherhood Curriculum, Workbook, First Edition. Sophia Murphy, Dan Griffin, and Harrison Crawford.

Common Man Rules

While this program is focused on moms and the Woman Rules, it is important to recognize that there is messaging and pressure put on men regarding masculinity, which we call the Man Rules. Men and women both have rules for how they "should" think, act, and feel to fit the gender scripts that our culture has for both sexes. The Man Rules are just as powerful and can be just as harmful to men as the Woman Rules can be to women. Therefore, we want to make sure to understand the common Man Rules because that knowledge can help you better empathize with any men in your life. Some of the most common Man Rules we hear when we discuss the topic are below:

- Don't cry
- Don't ask for help
- Don't show emotions
- Don't lost control/Always be in control
- Don't be weak
- Don't back down
- Don't be vulnerable
- Don't be a wuss/sissy/etc.
- Don't be gay
- Don't be a girl
- Man up
- Have as much sex as possible, whenever possible, with as many hot and different chicks as possible, with as little connection as possible, with as big of a dick as possible
- Be a provider
- Be a protector
- Integrity
- Responsibility
- Discipline
- Courage
- Don't hit or disrespect women

The Impact of the Rules of Gender

Consider the ways that the Man Rules are as limiting to boys and men as the Woman Rules are for women and girls. Also, you might notice that the Man Rules are nearly complete opposites of the Woman Rules. If you think about it, this means that both women and men are only "allowed" to act in ways that are opposite of each other, and both sides must miss out on the full human experience to conform to our culture's ideas about gender.

Men are taught to be powerful, in control, assertive, and to lead. But don't dare show their feelings, don't care about relationships, never let their guard down or show vulnerability. Women, on the other hand, are taught to be nurturing, caring, to seek meaningful relationships, and to value connection with others. But don't try to be a leader, don't be assertive because it comes across as bossy, always worry about your weight, and always put others first. You can see how both sides miss out on some important parts of the human experience.

Men are taught to present as cool, in charge, and aren't allowed to show tenderness or gentleness for fear of being perceived as "weak." Because they are not taught to value softness, this often negatively impacts their relationships, especially with women. They may look to women for caretaking and undervalue their internal traits as compared to their external traits or what they can "do" for them.

Part of the significance of the Man Rules lies in how they influence and impact male caregivers to your children – your significant other, coparent, or any other caregivers - so being aware of these Rules can help improve your understanding of some of the ways that men in your life behave.

Descriptions of Common Family Roles

After going through the Family Sculpture activity, you should have a better understanding of some of the common roles that exist within many families. Here are the descriptions that were covered today so you have them to reference later.

Hero: The Hero is most often the first-born child in a family. The Hero takes on the role of making the family look good. She usually gets the best grades, excels in sports, and follows the rules of the family. She feels a lot of pressure to be perfect.

She is expected to always represent the family in a positive way. The Hero can be at risk for emotional abuse due to significant and sometimes inappropriate responsibilities placed on her.

Scapegoat: The Scapegoat is usually the second-born child in a family. Since the Hero is the one who excels at everything, the Scapegoat must find other ways to get attention in the family. She usually figures out that she can do this by acting out. She rebels and does not follow the rules of the family. In doing so, she distracts attention away from the real causes of the family's dysfunction – the unhealthy relationship between Dad and Mom. The Scapegoat usually turns to people outside the family for any sense of connection. She is more social with peers but is also more susceptible to peer pressure. The Scapegoat can be vulnerable to physical abuse due to her acting-out tendencies.

Lost Child: The Lost Child is usually the third-born child in the family. The Hero and the Scapegoat already get the lion's share of attention in the family, so the Lost Child tends to fade into the background as she cannot compete. She tends to keep to herself and is careful not to cause problems. She often focuses on reading, computers, video games, and other activities she can do on her own. The Lost Child can be at risk for sexual abuse due to her isolation.

Mascot: The Mascot is usually the last-born child. She tends to fill the role of family jester. She often gets attention by using humor or charm, but she can also be hyperactive. In healthy families, she tends to be well-cared for because she has many other siblings to play with and because by their last child many parents have relaxed their parenting styles. However, in high-stress families, each additional child is viewed as a burden to the family. She is often more vulnerable to physical abuse due to her hyperactivity and the increased stress in the family.

Create Your Family of Origin Collage

Use the following prompts to help you create your Family of Origin Collage:

1. Who will you include in your project? Which parent(s), caregivers, or siblings (if any)? Any extended family members?
2. What will you depict them doing? How can you depict what was going on in your family at the time?

3. How do the Woman Rules show up in your project?

4. Consider which family members you want to be next to one another, or if you feel any members need to be separate from one another.

5. Will you use many different colors, only a few, or no color?

Place of Peace Relaxation Exercise – Family Version

This version of the Place of Peace exercise allows you to consider family members you do or do not want to include in your Place of Peace. Remember, you are invited to ignore any worries about how "good" you are at going through guided imagery, and instead focus on the power that this exercise offers you to choose who you include in your peaceful place.

1. Take a deep breath in while you silently count to four. One, two, three, four.

2. Now breathe out slowly for four. One, two, three, four.

3. Remember to breathe from your abdomen. Breathe in again. One, two, three, four.

4. And out again. One, two, three, four.

5. Now picture in your mind your place of peace. See that place in your mind.

6. Keep breathing slowly and deeply.

7. Let the muscles in your face relax.

8. Let your brow relax.

9. Let your jaw relax.

10. Let your neck and your shoulders relax.

11. Imagine all the tension draining out of them. Let it go.

12. Let your hands and arms go limp next to you.

13. Let your middle relax – your chest and your abdomen.

14. Keep breathing in and out.

15. Let your hips and your legs relax.

16. Let your feet relax.

17. Relax your whole body and imagine yourself in that favorite, safe place. Now imagine there is a giant bubble surrounding your place of peace. The bubble keeps you safe. It keeps the good inside, and the bad outside.

18. You get to choose what enters the bubble into your place of peace and what stays outside.

19. Now imagine any family members, including none, who you would like to invite into your place of peace. See them coming through the bubble to join you inside.

20. Next imagine any family members, including none, who you would like to leave outside your bubble, keeping them outside your place of peace. See them leaving your bubble so that only the people you choose are inside.

21. You feel completely supported inside your place of peace. You are fully in control of who comes in and who remains outside.

22. Breathe in to let in the safety and love you feel for those family members joining you.

23. Breathe out to push out any pain or discomfort.

24. Breathe in calm.

25. Breathe out any pain or discomfort.

Repeat the breathing process several more times.

Into Action

Continue working on your Family of Origin Collage and complete it before the next meeting. You will be asked to share it with another mom at the beginning of the next meeting. It may be helpful to work on it a little each night to keep any pressure off finishing it in time. Remember you can use the prompts beginning on page 84 in this workbook to help you create your project.

Practical & Tactical

Think back to the children's family roles that were discussed in today's meeting: The Hero, the Scapegoat, the Lost Child, and the Mascot. Answer the following questions:

1. Which role do you feel was the primary role you took on in your family of origin? It is very likely that you identified with multiple roles but there was probably one that showed up the most, especially as a child.

2. What purpose did you serve the family in taking on your primary role? What did your family get out of it? What did you get out of it?

3. What did your primary role cost you?

4. Describe the ways you continue to take on your primary childhood role in your relationships today.

5. Are there behaviors that help you still? Are there any that cost you still?

6. Do you see any of these roles playing out in how your children behave?

None of this is meant to shame you or be negative; it is just about bringing awareness and conscious choice to your behaviors. YOU get to decide what to do with that awareness.

Bonus: Have a conversation with someone in your family about your experiences. This could be your partner or someone from your immediate family. Ask them what role they think you played growing up and/or currently play in the family. Ask them what role they might identify with the most. Discuss how these roles may still show up for you both in your relationships today.

Summary

Our past influences our present. This may sound simple, but it's true. This meeting helped you explore your history within your family of origin, learn some new ways to interpret your experiences in your family growing up, and recognize how those experiences influence you today. That influence may have resulted in you falling into similar family patterns like what you saw growing up, or it may have pushed you to do something different from your family of origin. Either option can be both good and bad. But the key to understanding the positives and negatives is awareness.

Awareness of those influences allows you to intentionally choose your behavior. Maybe you will choose to keep doing what you have been doing because it is healthy. Or maybe you see that you have been acting in ways that aren't helpful to you or your children, and you now have the awareness and intention to do something differently. This is a gift you can give to yourself and your children so they do not end up having a similar experience to the one you had, if that is something you want them to avoid.

This is another meeting that may have been challenging for you, as many moms had very difficult experiences in their families of origin. If this is you, know that you are not alone. Also, remember that you have access to many tools and skills that can help you manage any challenging emotions or reactions that come from what was discussed in this meeting.

Father of Mine

The primary focus of this meeting is to explore your relationship with your father. Many of us do not recognize our fathers as imperfect men with their own problems, insecurities, pain, and even trauma. Regardless of whether you liked your father or even knew him, he had a profound impact on your life. The hope is that this meeting will give you some new perspectives on your father's life. You will also have an opportunity to communicate (to other moms in the group) some of what you may have never shared with your father to help you in healing or simply celebrating your relationship with him.

The goals of Meeting 9 are:

1. To explore your relationship with your father or father figure.

2. To recognize the role your father played in shaping your life today.

3. To look at your relationship with your father, how it influences how you treat men today, and its influence on how you parent your children.

Amazing Moms! Motherhood Curriculum, Workbook, First Edition. Sophia Murphy, Dan Griffin, and Harrison Crawford.
© 2026 Sophia Murphy, Dan Griffin, and Harrison Crawford. Published 2026 by John Wiley & Sons, Inc.

Sharing Your Family of Origin Project

Use the following prompts to help you present your project to your dyad partner:

- Introduce the family members in your project to your dyad partner.

- Describe what made you choose this specific time in your life to use for your project.

- If you are not in your family project, why did you not include yourself?

- Describe why you placed family members next to or apart from one another.

- Describe your reasons for using the color(s) you used.

The exploration of your relationship with your father and/or father figure is critical for your own growth to become the best mother you can be. Many people have a "father wound" that stems from experiences with their father, whether their father was in their life or not. Sometimes the wounds can come from a father figure who was not your biological father. No matter your experience or your relationship, exploring this in depth is part of becoming a conscious mother. If you have experienced a father wound, this can give you the nudge to begin looking at healing it.

Your relationship with your father taught you many things: you learned what is expected of fathers, how fathers are "supposed" to behave, and what makes a "good" or "bad" father. You learned how men treat women and even how you might expect a man to treat you. Next, you are invited to do an activity about the expectations society has of fathers.

It is likely that many of these expectations are similar to the Man Rules you identified during the last meeting. Many of these expectations were also likely passed down to you from your father, or a father figure in your life.

Relationships with Our Fathers – Discussion Questions

Use the following questions to discuss your relationship with your father/s. Every mom should answer each question before moving to the next one. Make sure each of you answers each question in your discussion.

Amazing Moms! Motherhood Curriculum

1. How would you describe your relationship with your father or father figure when you were a child?

2. How would you describe your relationship with your father or father figure when you were an adolescent?

3. If your father or father figure is still alive, how would you describe your relationship with him now? If he is no longer alive, how was your relationship when he died?

4. In what ways did your experiences with your father or father figure shape how you parent? Which of these are you proud of and which of these would you like to stop?

5. In what ways did your experiences with your father or father figure shape your expectations of the other men in your life (spouse, coparent, and/or father figures for your child/children)? How are these expectations helping or hurting your experience as a mother?

This next meditation exercise is designed to help you focus on positive thoughts of love and kindness. There are different versions of the Loving Kindness Meditation throughout the *Amazing Moms!* program. If you are participating in group meetings, you'll go through some father- and mother-specific versions. However, for simplicity's sake, the version that follows is a more general one that allows you to focus on any relationship you choose. You may not feel love or kindness toward that person at this moment, but this exercise is merely an invitation to practice what it would be like to offer those feelings.

Loving Kindness Meditation

1. Get into a relaxed position, for example, seated or lying down.
2. Take a deep breath through your nose.
3. Hold it.
4. Now, slowly let it go through your mouth.
5. Let's do that one more time, please.
6. Take a deep breath through your nose.
7. Hold it.
8. Now, slowly let it go through your mouth.
9. Continue breathing deeply, slowly, and steadily.
10. Focus on feeling kindness toward yourself. Move past any thoughts of doubt that come up.
11. Say the following phrases to yourself, not out loud but in your head.
    d. May I be happy.
    e. May I be healthy.
    f. May I know peace.
12. Continue breathing slowly and deeply.
13. Now think of a relationship you have struggled with. Picture that person in your mind.
14. Imagine that person as a child, before you knew them, before any conflict with them.
15. Say the following phrases to the image of this person you have in your mind:
    a. I wish you to be happy.
    b. I wish you to be healthy.
    c. I wish you to know peace.

16. Continue breathing deeply and slowly, breathing in kindness, and breathing out pain and conflict.

Into Action: Letter to Your Father

Write a letter to your father. You won't mail this letter and you don't have to share it with him, but it will be a chance for you to put on paper what you've always wanted to tell him. Take some time to think about what you'd really like to say. If you had a stepfather or grandfather who was the primary male figure in your life and you would prefer to write a letter to him, that's fine.

Spelling and grammar don't count; just write from your heart. Try to say the things that you have always wanted to say but were never able to.

You don't have to do this in letter form, either. There are many ways to express yourself. You can create drawings that reflect what you want to say, or you could create a collage, a poem, a spoken-word piece, a rap, or share a song that expresses what you would like to communicate.

You may use the space provided to write or draw your message to your father. If you prefer, or if you think that you will need more space, do your writing or drawing on a separate piece of paper.

You may choose to share this letter with your father/father figure; however, carefully consider whether you and he are ready to have this experience. If you feel you would like to share your letter, consider waiting for a period of one month. Sit with the idea, and if you still feel that way in one month then explore sharing it. Perhaps even consider sharing it with a trusted friend, mentor, or sponsor and get their feedback.

The bottom line about the letter is this: Whether you do it as a letter or some form of art, you cannot do the wrong project, but you can do the EASY project. We instead encourage you to challenge yourself with this exercise.

Here are some prompts to get you thinking. These may help you write your letter:

1. If your father had a problem with mental health issues, alcohol, other drugs, or any other addiction, how did this impact you?
2. What did you learn about men from your father or father figure?
3. What did you learn about women and mothers from your father or father figure?
4. Do you hold any anger or resentment toward your father or father figure?

Dear. . .

Practical & Tactical

Write a letter from your father to you. Write yourself the letter that you wish your father would write or would have written if your father is no longer alive. Consider the following questions when writing this letter:

- What have you always wanted to hear your father say to you?
- Is there anything he could write to you to improve the relationship you have/had with him?

Dear. . .

Summary

Meeting 9 continued exploring your relationships with family and caregivers, specifically your father or father figure. For many moms, exploring this relationship can be quite painful, sad, or angering. Many moms have a "father wound" that exists and influences them as women and as mothers. This meeting offered you a chance to explore that father wound by recognizing that your father or father figure was merely a man, with flaws and challenges, who made mistakes. Taking a detailed look at the relationship you had with him, whether he was involved in your life or not, is part of the healing process and builds insight into how you show up as a mother. Perhaps you are like your father or father figure. Perhaps you do things very differently. Either way, your relationship with your father influences your choices.

Exploring your relationship with your father can be difficult, so you are strongly advised to check in with yourself and practice the skills you have learned to make sure you take care of yourself in healthy ways. This is especially true as you take the time to do the Into Action work of writing a letter to your father. It is best to give yourself time to complete the letter, so starting on it early is advised to allow yourself the option to take breaks and come back to it if you need to.

Completing this exploration is a big step on the path to becoming a conscious mother, and the mother you desire to be!

MEETING 10

Mothers

The primary focus of this meeting is to explore your relationship with your mother. Many of us do not recognize our mothers as imperfect women with their own problems, insecurities, pain, and even trauma. Regardless of whether you liked your mother or even knew her, she had a profound impact on your life just as you do - and always will - with your children. How you related to your mother and how she treated you is connected to how you relate to other women and treat them. The hope of this meeting is to give you a new perspective on your mother's life. You will also have an opportunity to communicate to other moms in the group what you may have never shared with your mother to help you in healing or simply celebrating your relationship with her.

The goals of Meeting 10 are:

1. To share with the group your letter to your father.
2. To explore your relationship with your mother.
3. To recognize the role your mother played in shaping your life today.
4. To identify the expectations you and others place upon mothers and how that impacts your parenting.

Amazing Moms! Motherhood Curriculum, Workbook, First Edition. Sophia Murphy, Dan Griffin, and Harrison Crawford.
© 2026 Sophia Murphy, Dan Griffin, and Harrison Crawford. Published 2026 by John Wiley & Sons, Inc.

Mother Rules and Expectations

The chances are your mother did most of the child rearing. Regardless of the relationship you had with your mother, your mother was likely to have been the constant in your life. Maybe your mom raised you with little to no help from your father or any other man. Maybe you even had two mothers. On the other hand, you may have had a mother who was not there for you or who abandoned you completely. Or she may have been abusive and violent.

The ways in which your father or other men treated your mother likely had a significant impact on you, whether you are aware of it or not. Often, this was influenced by your perception of how you believed your mother was *allowing* herself to be treated. Both factors affected your thoughts and assumptions about your mother and women in general. More importantly, they affected how you treat yourself, allow yourself to be treated, and even how you treat other women. These ideas are part of The Water, meaning you may not even be aware of them. A reminder: this is not your own doing, but rather a result of the Water you have been in your whole life. Recognize any feelings of guilt or shame that may come up for you and practice the tools you have learned to help address those feelings. The information you are learning here is meant to help you gain awareness of what influences you to allow you the conscious choice to do something different.

This next activity gives you an opportunity to explore what "rules" there are for mothers and the different expectations that tend to be placed upon mothers.

Mother Rules and Expectations

You may use the following space to take notes during this interactive lecture:

1. When you think of a "bad" mother, what do you think of? Identify traits, behaviors, and weaknesses that you associate with "bad" mothers.

Amazing Moms! Motherhood Curriculum

2. When you think of a "good" mother, what do you think of? Again, you can identify behaviors, strengths, and traits that you feel exemplify what makes a "good" mother.

3. When you think of your own mother, which responses to the previous two questions apply? Why?

Answer this next question in your subgroup, and feel free to take notes here:

4. How do the lessons you learned about women and mothers impact your parenting? How do they impact your relationship with the father of your children?

Now that you have had a chance to explore the rules and expectations for mothers, it is time to delve more into your relationship with your own mother and/or mother figure. No matter what your experience or your relationship is, or was, with your mother, exploring it in-depth is important to give you perspective.

Relationships with Our Mothers – Discussion Questions

Use the following questions to discuss your relationships with your mothers. Every mom should answer each question before moving to the next one.

1. How would you describe your relationship with your mother or mother figure when you were a child?

2. How would you describe your relationship with your mother or mother figure when you were an adolescent?

3. If your mother or mother figure is still alive, how would you describe your relationship with her now? If she is no longer alive, how was your relationship when she died?

4. How did your father or other men treat your mother or mother figure?

5. In what ways do you parent like your mother or mother figure?

6. In what ways do you avoid parenting like your mother or mother figure?

Into Action: Letter to Your Mother

Write a letter to your mother. You won't mail this letter and you don't have to share it with her, but it will be a chance for you to put on paper what you've always wanted to tell her. Take some time to think about what you'd really like to say. If you had a stepmother or grandmother who was the primary female figure in your life and you would prefer to write a letter to her, that is fine. It is okay to feel anger or resentment toward your mother. It doesn't mean you love her any less or take away from the fact that she was there for you (if that was your experience). Nobody is perfect but if that resentment and anger are getting in the way of your relationships with others, isn't it worth it to explore it?

Spelling and grammar don't count; just write from your heart. Try to say the things that you have always wanted to say but were never able to.

You don't have to do this in letter form, either. There are many ways to express yourself. You can create drawings that reflect what you want to say, or you could create a collage, a poem, a spoken-word piece, a rap, or share a song that expresses what you would like to communicate.

You may use the space provided to write or draw your message to your mother. If you prefer, or if you think that you will need more space, do your writing or drawing on a separate piece of paper.

You may choose to share this letter with your mother/mother figure; however, carefully consider whether you and she are ready to have this experience. If you feel you would like to share your letter, consider waiting for a period of one month. Sit with the idea, and if you still feel that way in one month then explore sharing it. Perhaps even consider sharing it with a trusted friend, mentor, or sponsor and get their feedback.

The bottom line about the letter is this: Whether you do it as a letter or some form of art, you cannot do the wrong project, but you can do the EASY project. We instead encourage you to challenge yourself with this exercise.

Here are some prompts to get you thinking. These may help you write your letter:

1. If your mother or mother figure had a problem with mental health issues, alcohol, other drugs, or any other addiction, how did this impact you?
2. What did you learn about being a woman from your mother or mother figure?
3. What did you learn about being a mother from your mother or mother figure?
4. Do you hold any anger or resentment toward your mother or mother figure?
5. Do you think your mother or mother figure is, or would be, proud or disappointed in the mother you have become?

Practical & Tactical

Have a conversation with your sister(s), female friends, mother, or any other woman in your life about the expectations that are put on mothers. Discuss what you learned during this meeting and use this as an opportunity to gain more insight into her feelings on this topic and support you in exploring yours in more depth. Here are several questions to help you in your discussion:

- What do you feel are the expectations put on you as a mother?
- How realistic do you think they are? How realistic do you think the number of expectations is?
- How do you feel if you judge yourself to have fallen short on an expectation?
- Is there any way we can help ourselves to ease the expectations put on us as women and mothers?

Summary

This meeting gave you an opportunity to share your letter to your father, and hopefully, that was a valuable experience for you. We often think that nobody knows what we have gone through, but that activity often helps moms see that others have had similar experiences and that there is a benefit in sharing those experiences together to promote healing. If your relationship was positive, then sharing that with the group was a beacon of hope for the other moms to recognize that they can be the ones to create that positive relationship with their children now.

You then shifted to discussing your relationship with your mother or mother figure. Like the previous meeting, this was a chance to look at your mother not as a divine being, although you may still view her that way, but as a human being with flaws, pain, and challenges of her own. Additionally, thinking about all the expectations that get put upon mothers can be an eye-opening exercise for many who realize just how unrealistic it is to pile all those expectations onto mothers.

Your opportunity to write a letter to your mother is just as important as the letter you wrote to your father. It's likely that this will be a much different letter than your father's letter. However, taking the chance to express yourself to your mother this way, whether you end up ever sharing the contents with her or not, is part of your journey to recognize what influences you and to express your thoughts and feelings about your experiences in one of your most influential relationships. As always, please make sure you check in with yourself and take care of yourself if any part of this becomes difficult for you. You are doing the hard work so it's important to remind yourself that this is the work of a conscious mother.

Healthy Relationships – Boundaries, Communication, and Conflict

This meeting covers multiple important topics that are intricately connected to having healthy relationships. At its core, being a healthy mother involves developing and maintaining healthy relationships with others, especially your children. That may seem obvious, but the challenge is that our society still does not truly or adequately prepare women to be able to navigate relationships in healthy ways.

You will learn about boundaries and how to practice setting healthy boundaries with others. There are different types of boundaries, and you will be exposed to four main types. A critical component of setting boundaries, and for developing healthy relationships in general, is communication. This meeting will provide some guidance around four basic styles of communication.

Finally, you will put everything together in an exploration of how to manage conflict. There is no such thing as a conflict-free family. Learning to deal effectively with conflict is an incredibly important skill for you individually, but also as you raise your children. Conflict often involves mistakes. However, repairing *after* conflict is just as important as trying to use healthy skills *during* the conflict.

Amazing Moms! Motherhood Curriculum, Workbook, First Edition. Sophia Murphy, Dan Griffin, and Harrison Crawford.
© 2026 Sophia Murphy, Dan Griffin, and Harrison Crawford. Published 2026 by John Wiley & Sons, Inc.

The goals of Meeting 11 are:

1. To share your letter to your mother and experience other moms sharing theirs.
2. To understand different types of boundaries.
3. To better understand different styles of communication.
4. To look at socialization patterns for women through the lens of boundaries and communication styles.
5. To learn how to engage in healthy conflict and to model this for your children.

This meeting is the first with some new breathing and grounding exercises that are part of the check-in process. You will find those new exercises on the coming pages. You can also find them at the back of the workbook in the appendix where all the grounding, relaxation, and breathing exercises are in one spot.

Full-Body Breathing

Begin in a standing position, making sure you have space in front of you for this exercise.

- Standing up straight, take a deep breath in for six counts through your nose. One, two, three, four, five, six.
- Hold your breath for a count of four. One, two, three, four.
- Exhale your full breath through your mouth for six counts. One, two, three, four, five, six.
- Now, slowly bend forward at the waist, keeping your knees slightly bent, and let your arms dangle down toward the floor. Bend as far as you are comfortable with.
- As you inhale slowly and deeply, return to a standing position by rolling up slowly, lifting your head last. Do this over the course of six counts.
- When you reach your full standing position, hold your breath for a count of four.
- Exhale slowly as you return to your starting position, bending forward from the waist. Do this for six counts.
- Repeat the process again. Bend at the waist, with your arms dangling toward the ground. Slowly take a deep breath and roll up to a standing position over six counts.
- Hold your breath for a count of four at the top.
- Exhale slowly as you roll back down to your starting position over six counts.

Now go through this routine two more times on your own. Make sure to do this slowly to help avoid any pain or injuries. Notice how it feels to stretch while you breathe.

Optional: If you have any pain issues, especially in your back, the following can be a less physically demanding version of the exercise.

- Start with your arms hanging down against your sides.
- As you begin to take a deep breath in for a count of six, slowly raise your arms in an arc until they meet above your head outstretched. The motion is similar to doing a jumping jack.
- Hold your breath and your arms outstretched for a count of four.
- As you exhale for a count of six, bring your arms down along the same arc until they are back at your sides.

This exercise combines the physical element of stretching with the same breathing skills as some of the other exercises. It is a useful exercise to do in the morning to help stretch out stiff muscles and open your breathing passages.

Progressive Muscle Relaxation

The exercise involves tensing different muscle groups. If you have pain in any area of your body and you feel that tensing that area would be painful, skip the tension part of that muscle group and focus on the relaxation of the muscles.

1. Begin by taking a deep breath for a count of four. Notice the feeling of air filling up your lungs. One, two, three, four.
2. Hold your breath for a count of four. One, two, three, four.
3. Release the breath slowly for a count of four and let the tension out of your body. One, two, three, four.
4. Pause for a count of four. One, two, three, four.
5. Even slower now, take another deep breath this time for a count of six. One, two, three, four, five, six.
6. Hold it for a count of six. One, two, three, four, five, six.
7. Slowly release the breath over a count of six, feeling the tension leaving your body. One, two, three, four, five, six.

8. Now, move your attention to your feet. Begin to tense your feet by curling your toes and the arch of your foot. Hold the tension and notice what it feels like. *(5-second pause)*

9. Release the tension in your feet and notice the new feeling of relaxation.

10. Next, shift your focus to your lower legs. Tense the muscles in your calves. Hold them tightly and pay attention to the feeling of tension. *(5-second pause)*

11. Release the tension from your lower legs. Again, notice the feeling of relaxation. Remember to continue taking deep breaths.

12. Next, tense the muscles of your upper leg and pelvis and hold it. You can do this by squeezing your thighs together. Make sure you feel tension without going to the point of strain. *(5-second pause)*

13. Now release and feel the tension leave your muscles.

14. Begin to tense your stomach and chest. You can do this by sucking in your stomach. Squeeze harder and hold the tension. *(5-second pause)*

15. Release the tension. Allow your body to go limp. Notice the feeling of relaxation.

16. Continue taking deep breaths. Breathe in slowly, noticing how it feels as the air fills your lungs.

17. Release the air slowly, feeling it leave your lungs on its way out.

18. Next, tense the muscles in your back by bringing your shoulders together behind you. Hold them tightly. Tense them as hard as you can without straining and keep holding. *(5-second pause)*

19. Release the tension from your back. Feel it slowly leaving your body, being replaced by a feeling of relaxation. Notice how different your body feels when you allow it to relax.

20. Tense your arms all the way from your hands to your shoulders. Make a fist and squeeze all the way up your arm. Hold it. *(5-second pause)*

21. Release the tension from your arms and shoulders and notice how your arms feel limp and at ease.

22. Move up to your neck and your head. Tense your face and neck by distorting the muscles around your eyes and mouth. *(5-second pause)*

23. Release the tension. Again, notice the new feeling of relaxation.

24. Finally, tense your entire body. Tense your feet, legs, stomach, chest, arms, head, and neck. Tense harder, without straining, and hold that tension. *(5-second pause)*

25. Now release and allow your body to go completely limp. Pay attention to that feeling of relaxation, and how different it is from the feeling of tension.

26. Begin to wake your body up by slowly shifting your arms and legs.

Holding tension in the muscle and then releasing it can create a feeling of full relaxation in that muscle. By going through all the major muscle groups, you can practice removing the tension from the whole body. Additionally, shifting your focus to different parts of your body is a grounding practice by keeping your mind in the present – the "here and now" – and noticing sensations in your body. As you practice this exercise, you will likely see an improvement in your ability to truly feel the relaxation effect.

Important Definition: Boundary

"A boundary is something that delineates where one person ends and the other begins. This can be an external boundary such as who you let touch you and be in your 'bubble'. This can also be an internal boundary such as your thoughts and feelings and how much you're able to, or struggle to, separate yourself from someone else."

– Dr. Sophia Murphy, DBH, LPC

The Four Types of Boundaries

1. *None*: When someone never says no, "goes with the flow," and struggles to separate their emotions and thoughts from others. They may be easily swayed by others and often feel overwhelmed by others.

2. *Rigid*: When someone walls themselves off to others. They struggle to take feedback or change beliefs, even when the evidence says it would be helpful to do so. They may also avoid physical closeness, emotional closeness, or both with others.

3. *Damaged*: A combination of the first two types. This person may have no limits in some parts of their lives and then be overly rigid and withdraw or isolate themselves from others.

4. *Flexible or Healthy*: When someone is self-aware and intentional in their decision-making. This person can expand or contract their boundaries when they want to, and they make that choice mindfully. They can be vulnerable and open when they desire and understand themselves as separate from others in a way that supports individuality and connection.

Important Definition: Communication

"Communication is the way to share and receive information between multiple parties." – Dr. Sophia Murphy, DBH, LPC

Communication Styles

The following are four of the most common styles of communication, described from the perspective of mothers:

- *Passive*: Moms who are passive communicators put the needs, wants, and feelings of others ahead of their own. This could be their children's, spouse's, or others in their lives. Moms with a passive style of communication generally go along with others to the point where they tend to agree to things they don't want to. This is more than a mom simply putting her children's needs first in an appropriate and healthy way. It involves avoiding communicating her own needs or important boundaries in order to avoid conflict, to her own detriment. Moms who are passive communicators may believe they are being treated unfairly but will not say anything about it. Passive communication seeks to avoid conflict at all costs, and the cost is usually highest for the mom who is being passive.

- *Aggressive*: Moms who are aggressive communicators often express their feelings and opinions with little regard for whom they are communicating with. This can be a dangerous form of communication. These moms are focused on being "right" or making sure their needs are met above anybody else's, including their children's. Aggressive communication can involve yelling, threatening, blaming, and even violent behavior. Unfortunately, this type of communication is often rewarded in the short term because others back down out of fear. Aggressive communication can give a false impression that it gets the job done, but the damaging effects, especially with children, are being proven more and more as studies show. Despite getting what they want, aggressive communicators experience real costs to their relationships.

- *Passive–aggressive*: Moms who use passive-aggressive communication appear passive on the surface but have little intent of giving in to the other person. They respond by acting out in more subtle or indirect ways. They may agree to do something, and then purposefully do it poorly, complain the whole time, or simply not follow through at all. For example, a mom might agree to give or do something for her child with no intention of following through. Or she might go

Amazing Moms! Motherhood Curriculum

along with his child's wish, like doing an activity, but complain about it the whole time. Sarcasm is often a sign of passive-aggressive communication. Moms who use this style appear cooperative but purposefully do things to undermine, annoy, or disrupt.

- *Assertive*: Moms who communicate assertively clearly state their opinions, feelings, and needs while still respecting their own boundaries and those of others. The assertive communicator does not want to avoid conflict at all costs, but she also doesn't want to overpower the other person to "win." This style is about making your needs known, but also listening to and respecting the needs of the person with whom you're communicating. Moms who use this style use "I" messages, which means they take ownership of their feelings and their role in the interaction. For example, a mom might say to her child, "I feel sad when I ask you to do something multiple times and it still doesn't get done," or "I feel frustrated when I am trying to talk and keep getting interrupted." This type of communication does not blame or shame the other person. This is the least emotion-driven form of communication of the four styles, and the most effective in the long term.

Defining Boundary and Communication Styles

The goal of having healthy relationships may seem an obvious one, but it can often be one of the hardest parts of being a mom and one of the most challenging tasks you face as a woman.

The challenges women face with relationships often come back to the Woman Rules. Our culture promotes a narrative that women must be solely focused on others, to ignore their own needs, always say "yes" and be able to do it all and do it perfectly. There definitely are women who approach relationships that way. However, when women approach relationships this way, they often struggle with their own boundaries and styles of communication.

There is an easy way to think of the difference between healthy and unhealthy styles: Healthy styles are ones that have more pros than cons, allow us more of what we want and less of what we don't, and are more sustainable over time. Unhealthy styles have the opposite effects.

Intersections of the Styles of Communication, Boundaries, and Conflict

All relationship interactions are based on the intersections of these two factors: how committed we are to ourselves and how committed we are to the relationship. This goes for all relationships including familial, romantic, friendship, or even work relationships. Each quadrant of the image below represents a relationship style and an approach to conflict and negotiation based on these intersections. For women, there is often a distinct, internal conflict where we feel torn between ourselves and the relationship. As moms, this can be even harder when we feel forced to sacrifice ourselves for our children or our relationship. Even when part of that sacrifice is important or necessary, it can become unmanageable.

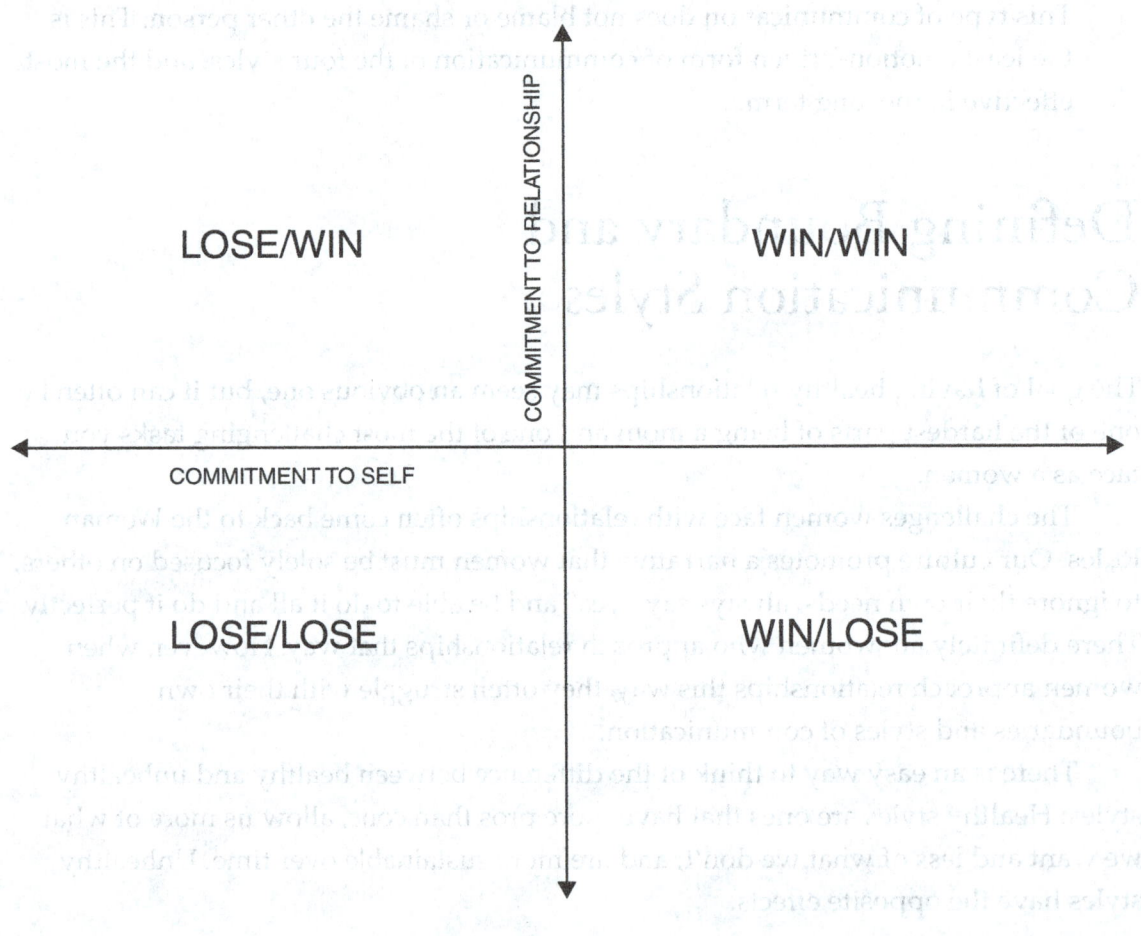

Subgroup Discussion: Pros and Cons

Please answer the following questions in your small groups, and feel free to take notes below.

1. Identify the boundary style that likely exists in and reinforces each of the four quadrants of interactional styles? Why did you select the one you did?

2. Identify the communication style that likely exists in and reinforces each of the four quadrants of interaction styles? Why did you select the one you did?

3. What are the potential pros/cons of each?
   a. Lose/lose:
   b. Win/lose:
   c. Lose/win:
   d. Win/win:

Subgroup Discussion: The Rules and How to Move Toward the "Win/Win"

1. Which section of the Win/Lose diagram is most likely a result of the Woman Rules?

2. Which section of the diagram is most likely a result of the Man Rules?

3. Which pair of boundary styles and communication styles (which quadrant) resonates most with you and your role as a mother and partner? Why?

4. What can you identify as gains and losses in your life and relationships because of your boundary and communication style combination? Why?

Improving your ability to communicate effectively during times of conflict or when you feel yourself having a strong reaction is something that will benefit you in every relationship, not just as a mother. Additionally, the more you work at this and practice healthier boundaries, communication, and conflict styles, the better able you are to be a positive role model for your children.

Into Action

Check in with your partner, coparent, or other caregivers about how you come across when you communicate, especially during times of conflict and especially with your children. Share the four communication styles with them.

1. Ask about the communication style they see you using, especially during conflict.

2. Ask for feedback about your body language, tone of voice, and volume.

3. Ask if there is anything you can do differently to improve your communication.

*** Understand that the other person's response is just feedback, and you can decide to take it or leave it. The feedback does not say anything about you personally, but it offers you an opportunity to get information you might not normally get. Asking for this information during times of calm (not during conflict) can help you game plan for future conflicts.

Practical and Tactical

Have a conversation with your children to come up with "Guidelines for Conflict" or "Fair Fighting Agreements" for conflict. It is also an excellent option to do this together with your children and your partner, coparent, or other caregivers. Come up with a list of rules you all agree to use during those times. Ideally, write or print the list out and hang it in a place where everyone can see it.

Examples of Guidelines/Agreements:

- Use "I" messages.
  - "I" messages take ownership and do not place blame. "I" messages start off with "I feel…" and then your feeling about the conflict. For example, instead of saying "You always interrupt me, and it irritates me," you could say, "I feel frustrated when I am trying to talk and keep getting interrupted." The "I" message does not involve pointing blame. The message has more chance of getting through.
- No blaming.
- No yelling.
- No use of force, threatening, or intimidating.
- No name-calling or put-downs.
- If one person needs to cool off, give him/her time to do so.
  - Come up with a neutral signal for when someone needs this cool-off.
    - We suggest a neutral word or hand signal.
    - Can be any neutral word that has no real meaning behind it, like "pineapple," or a hand signal like the "time out" signal you see in sports.
    - This is something you agree on together, ahead of time, and when someone uses it during the conflict the others know to respect that it means the person needs time to cool off.
    - This helps all involved understand that the person needs a break and isn't just walking away.
  - Make sure the length of time for the cool-off period is clear, so you can come back to trying to resolve the conflict and the cool-off period doesn't last indefinitely.
- One person gets to speak at a time. No interrupting.
- Everyone needs to sit down while talking.
- Only the current conflict gets discussed. This is not an opportunity to bring up old grievances. If there are things that need to be addressed, that is for a future time that can be chosen.

Summary

Similar to how the Woman Rules encourage hyperfocus on others with little awareness of your own wants or needs, the Rules also place very little emphasis on the importance of being a good communicator because women are expected to defer to others in all situations. The messages women get early are that "conflict is bad" and that saying "yes" is the most important thing a woman can do to avoid being selfish. These messages contribute to disconnection in relationships because many women are unable to be assertive without fearing negative feedback from others or a sense that they have broken one or more of the Woman Rules. We don't learn to be authentic, which actually makes us dishonest! We all deserve to learn to communicate more effectively and be honest with those we love.

This meeting was designed to give insight and provide tools to help improve your communication skills. You learned about the common communication styles and had a chance to explore the benefits and costs of each. You learned about various styles of boundaries and the common ways they show up with different communication styles, for better or worse. Understanding these connections can help you be more intentional in how you approach conflict and how you speak up for yourself. Revisit that idea multiple times so you can really get the hang of the process – it can help defuse difficult interactions. The process is listed in this workbook so you can review it whenever you need.

No discussion of communication skills is complete without shifting the perspective of conflict as "bad" to "helpful." We can all benefit from a "win/win" style. It is something you have probably heard many times, but today's meeting was designed to help you define and understand what "win/win" really means and requires. Hopefully, you see the ways you can use these skills with your children right away and begin to influence how they learn about managing conflict in their relationships.

Let's Talk About Sex

This is the first of two meetings dedicated to sex and sexuality. Given how The Woman Rules offer highly conflicting messages around femininity, being viewed as sexy or a sexual object, and what it means to be a sexual being, it is vital to explore these concepts in-depth. Your first reaction may be: "What does this have to do with me being a mother?" More than you may think. Set aside any doubts you have and commit to doing the exercises. After you've gone through both meetings, you will be able to connect this topic to your journey toward conscious motherhood.

This meeting begins with a very open and uncensored discussion about sex and sexuality – and the feelings connected to it that we often don't discuss as women and moms. Then you will learn about how sex and intimacy get confused a lot of the time, how women are not taught to enjoy sex outside of pleasing their partner (usually a male), and that to desire sex outside of love is a bad thing. Finally, you have an opportunity to reflect on everything you wish you had been told and taught about sex and sexuality as a child, knowing what you know now.

The goals of Meeting 12 are:

1. To identify common topics related to sex and the feelings associated with them.
2. To define sexuality and intimacy, understand the differences between them, and learn how the Woman Rules influence them.

Amazing Moms! Motherhood Curriculum, Workbook, First Edition. Sophia Murphy, Dan Griffin, and Harrison Crawford.

3. To consider what you wish you had been told or taught about these topics as a girl or young woman, especially knowing what you now know about sex, sexuality, and intimacy.

Sex and Feelings

Many women are heavily influenced by the Woman Rules when it comes to sex, especially when talking about sex with others. The Woman Rules around sex are some of the most rigid and limiting, and women are taught they should always be ready and receptive to sex. And, of course, every "real" woman must be completely focused on her partner with very little focus on her own needs.

The Woman Rules teach you that being sexual will bring you love and connection while you're also told not to be *too* sexual because you won't be taken seriously. Women are taught to use their bodies for the pleasure of someone else even if *they* don't experience pleasure in the process. This is true even if you hate your own body or learn to hate it through sexual experiences; your body's purpose is still to meet the needs of someone else. This, combined with the idea that you must give your body away to be loved, makes understanding healthy sex and sexuality even more problematic. Please remember this point: experiencing challenges with, or confusion about, your sexuality merely means you are human.

Important Concept: Purity Culture

"Women are often taught their sexuality is something that should be bottled up and shoved down. That encompasses everything from the way that they dress, the way that they interact with men, the way that they speak, the way that they view their own bodies, and their own sex drive." – Loeppky 2023

"Women are often taught in purity culture that they are supposed to be responsible for averting the male gaze, and if they receive unsolicited attention from that, that it is their fault. And it is a very harmful, vicious cycle of shame that can take a very long time to undo." – Hannah Mayderry, LMHC

From the Article *Purity Culture and its Effects on Mental* Health from www.verywellmind.comky

Purity Culture and Sexuality

Purity culture is one of the most dangerous toxins in the Water and has been around for millennia. Sadly, purity culture has found its way into religious teachings on sex and sexuality. While this has evolved to include politics and larger societal norms, the foundation of purity culture is rooted in the concept that sex outside of marriage is sinful. Currently, we see purity culture evidenced in a lack of sexual education, the inability to discuss sexuality for fear of being "unpure," and increased efforts to deny body autonomy to women. While there has been a more recent conversation and movement around purity culture, it's important to remember that purity culture has been a hallmark of the historical restrictions placed on women, their bodies, their sexuality, and their sense of self as part of their sexual identity. Purity culture is highly connected to oppression, shame, and judgment.

- What are some thoughts and feelings that come up when you think about purity culture?

- What are some of the consequences of purity culture for you as a woman?

- What were you taught about sex and sexuality *growing up*?

- What do you believe *today* about sex?

This next discussion gives you an opportunity to candidly explore your thoughts on your sexual self. Notice any discomfort you experience when going through these questions, but don't judge it. The discomfort could come from many sources and for many women, it often stems from the conflicting messages the Woman Rules have taught you about sex. If you can acknowledge your discomfort but continue with the activity, you may find that the discomfort begins to decrease. Practicing this non-judgmental noticing of discomfort will serve you well in the future; for example, when you begin having candid discussions with your children about sex and sexuality - a part of motherhood that is not often talked about in the open.

Subgroup Discussion: Sexual Satisfaction and Enjoyment

You are encouraged to discuss the following questions in your small groups and have the option to take notes below as well.

1. In what ways have the things you learned about sex growing up impacted your ability to enjoy sex? Are the impacts positive or negative?

2. On a scale of 1–5, how satisfied are you with your sexual self? Why did you choose that rating?

3. How do you think becoming a mother impacted your sexual self or enjoyment of sex?

4. What might be most helpful to improve your relationship with your sexual self?

5. How do you think this information about sex, socialization, and sexual wellness can impact how you parent your children?

What I Wish I Had Known

Using the space provided, write down the things you would like to tell the girlhood version of yourself about sex, sexuality, and intimacy. Hopefully, the discussion in this meeting has helped you gain new awareness, new information, and new perspectives on these concepts. At the very least, you certainly know more now than you did as a girl. Think about what you would want to share with that girlhood version of yourself, especially if you wish you had been better prepared or educated than you were.

Perhaps you would tell her all the things you were never told by your mother, father, or caregivers. Perhaps you would warn her about certain things. What about porn? It seems to be everywhere these days. What about respecting your body and other people's bodies? What about all the different feelings connected to sex and sexuality? You might want to share some positive experiences or aspects of your own sexuality. Maybe you would discuss some of the values you learned about sexuality.

Or perhaps you would explain to her how the Woman Rules will try to hijack her sexuality and how to recognize that. Write whatever comes to mind that you wish you had known when you were that young girl.

Things I would want to tell my younger self about sex, sexuality, and myself...

Into Action

Answer the following questions to explore more about your experiences with your sexual self. You will not be asked to share your answers with anyone, but you may do so if you choose to.

1. How comfortable are you setting boundaries around sex, specifically saying "no?"

2. How comfortable are you initiating sex and/or prioritizing your pleasure with sex?

3. What are you willing to change about how to navigate sex?

4. In what ways do you show intimacy with your children that has nothing to do with sexuality?

Practical & Tactical

It is interesting to consider how different our experiences of learning about sex, sexuality, and intimacy were when we were growing up. You may have had healthy, informed discussions with parents or parental figures. Or you may have had zero discussion with a parental figure and learned about these topics on your own or through friends, movies, and other media.

For this week's Practical & Tactical exercise, you are encouraged to find someone you trust and have a conversation with that person about their experience of learning about these topics when they were young. It is important to have this conversation with someone you feel is trusted and safe, and who feels the same way about you.

Here are some sample questions you could ask your trusted person:

1. Did your parents (or parental figures) ever sit you down and talk to you about the topics of sex, sexuality, and intimacy?
   a. If so, what was that like?
   b. If not, do you wish one or both had done so?
2. What do you wish you had learned about these topics when you were younger?
3. Do you think the depictions of sex, sexuality, and intimacy we see in the media are helpful or hurtful when it comes to young people learning about these topics? Why?
4. Would you be open to me sharing my answers to these questions with you?

The main idea behind this exercise is to begin to remove the stigma associated with having conversations about sex by helping you practice *healthy* conversations with others about these topics.

Summary

This meeting was meant to introduce the topics of sex, sexuality, and intimacy in ways that you may not have experienced before. The Woman Rules are a major factor in our views on sex, so undoing many of the messages you have received over time about sex from peers, the media, and others is a tough task, but one that is worth the time and effort. Recognizing that women are not just sexual objects and that they have a right to not only enjoy sex, but to set boundaries around sex is an important lesson. Again, the Woman Rules provide very conflicting messages around sex, specifically when conflated with love and used as a tool to gain connection. You also had a chance to consider the messages and lessons you wish someone had taught you as a child or adolescent to help you learn healthier ideas about these topics.

Why is this part of the motherhood curriculum? At the most basic level, sex is almost always required for motherhood, right? Creating a healthier understanding of sex, sexuality, and intimacy will help you feel more confident when it comes to raising your children and helping them navigate these topics. Being a mom who feels confident in that will offer your children safety and security and will help you feel better knowing that you can give them healthy messages versus the messages they will get outside of your parenting.

MEETING 13

Let's REALLY Talk About Sex

In this second meeting focused on sex and sexuality, you begin by having an open conversation about how you learned about sex as a child. There is also the very important conversation about consent that should be part of every discussion of sex and sexuality. The meeting ends with you having the opportunity to begin to develop your very own "sex talk" with your children for when you are ready to have that conversation

The goals of Meeting 13 are:

1. To practice healthy communication about sexuality in a safe space.
2. To improve your understanding of consent and the importance of teaching your children about consent.
3. To prepare for having "The Sex Talk" with your children.

Part of healthy sexuality involves understanding your own experience of learning about sex and sexuality growing up. You may or may not have had a healthy introduction to this, as every person's experience is often unique. However, part of conscious motherhood means recognizing the positives and negatives of what you went through and then making intentional choices about how you shape your children's experience learning about this topic. The questions in the next section will

Amazing Moms! Motherhood Curriculum, Workbook, First Edition. Sophia Murphy, Dan Griffin, and Harrison Crawford.
© 2026 Sophia Murphy, Dan Griffin, and Harrison Crawford. Published 2026 by John Wiley & Sons, Inc.

help you explore this further. Recognize that some of the questions might stir up some discomfort, bad memories, or be triggering. Remember the different skills you have learned to be able to cope with these feelings.

Let's Talk About Sex: Prompts for Subgroup Discussions

Answer the following questions in your subgroups:

1. Did your mother, father, or other caregiver talk to you about sex? If so, what was the conversation like? Do you want your kids to have a similar experience? Why or why not?

2. How old were you when you were first exposed to pornography? What was that like for you? What did it teach you about sex?

3. Would you want your kids to learn about pornography the same way you did? Why or why not?

4. With whom in your life would you feel comfortable having a "real" conversation about sex, if anybody? Have you had that conversation? How was it? What went well? What didn't go well?

5. What are you most worried about when it comes to talking to your children about sex, sexuality, and intimacy?

6. Would you be more worried about discussing sex with a daughter versus a son? Would it not matter to you? Why or why not?

Defining Consent

Consent is a critical topic to know about and to be able to teach to your children, both boys and girls. Our society has done a poor job of helping people clearly understand what consent is, who can and cannot give it, and how it applies to every person in any given sexual situation. Take the knowledge you gain during this next discussion and be sure to include consent in any conversations you have with your children.

1. How do you define consent?

2. How can someone get and/or give consent?

3. Who cannot consent?

Important Definition: Consent

"Consent is your agreement and permission to do a specific thing." – Andrew Smiler, PhD, author and psychologist

More Information on Consent

Getting consent:

- The clearest and safest form of consent is *verbal* consent, which is when someone gives clear verbal consent to do a specific thing.
- *Nonverbal* consent is another way to get consent, but it is not always clear, and the law does not always recognize nonverbal consent.

Who cannot consent?

Laws are different in every state. Make sure you know the laws where you live. Below are some general standards:

- Anyone under age 14 cannot consent to any sexual activity that involves a penis, vagina, clitoris, or anus.
- Anyone who is drunk, high, or otherwise impaired cannot legally provide consent.
- Mental and emotional vulnerabilities can also impair a person's ability to provide consent.
- Legal minors cannot consent to sexual activity if they are three or more years younger than the older partner, whether that older partner is a minor or not.

How does all of this relate to motherhood and this motherhood program? Being able to have healthy conversations with your children about these topics is one of the most important things you can do as a mother. Imagine all the anxiety, discomfort, anger, and pain you can help your children avoid by being the person to give them *healthy* information. Imagine the comfort they will feel knowing that you are "in their corner" and someone they can turn to for healthy guidance and support when dealing with these topics that our society likes to avoid approaching in healthy ways. Think of the gift you can give your children through your willingness to be there for them in this way.

Amazing Moms! Motherhood Curriculum

Preparing for "The Sex Talk"

There are many things you can choose to include in the conversations you have with your children about sex, sexuality, and intimacy. Here are some suggestions to help you organize what you want to say:

1. Topics I want to make sure I discuss with my children:

   a.

   b.

   c.

   d.

2. What topics am I afraid to discuss?

   a.

   b.

   c.

   d.

3. What topics feel uncomfortable or embarrassing for me to discuss even though I know they are important?

   a.

   b.

   c.

   d.

4. What might my children ask me?

   a.

   b.

   c.

   d.

5. What do I want to avoid?

   a.

   b.

   c.

   d.

6. What differences will/would there be in discussing this with a son versus a daughter? If applicable, why do you think there need to be differences?

Into Action

Continue working on what you would like to include in "The Sex Talk" with your children. Write down your ideas. Write examples of the things you want to say and think about some of the responses your children might have, or some of the questions they may ask you. Use the following space to keep track of your progress on this.

1. List the top three topics or "takeaways" you want to make sure you include in "The Sex Talk."
   a.
   b.
   c.

2. Write out more specific details about each of your top three – for example, what you would like to say about each one.
   a.

   b.

   c.

3. What can you do to make sure this is not a one-time conversation, but an ongoing dialogue with your children? How can you let them know that is what you hope for?
   a.

   b.

c.

d.

Practical & Tactical

It is never too early to begin to teach your children about consent, even if your children are not yet ready to learn about sex itself. One way to do this is to give them the *option* of hugging or kissing people, rather than telling them to do it. For example, when you see family or friends instead of telling your children, "Give _____ a hug and a kiss," you can give them a choice: "Do you want to give _____ a hug or a high five?" This is a basic way to begin to teach your children that they are in control of their own bodies, and whom they touch and when. Subtle messages like these can help shape their understanding of the importance of consent.

Suggestions for Healthy Conversations with Your Children

There are many different suggestions and ideas out there for how to start a healthy dialogue with your children about this important topic. The following is a list of a few suggestions, but it is not a comprehensive list. This is meant as a starting point to help you prepare for "The Sex Talk" with your children. You can follow as many or as few of these suggestions as you like, but they are meant to set you up for success.

1. Approach this with an understanding that ideally this is not just one "Sex Talk" with your children, but an opening for ongoing dialogue with them.

2. Offer a safe space. Let your children know that you are open to talking with them about any questions, concerns, and issues about these topics.

3. Be willing to admit you don't know something. Consider the possibility of researching it with your children. This shows your children that it is okay to not have all the answers, and equally okay to seek the answers from healthy sources.

4. Practice honesty, with discretion. Be truthful with your children, while understanding there should be some boundaries.

5. Roll with the discomfort. This is another good skill to model for your children. This does not mean pretending the discomfort is not there but rather acknowledging it and showing your children that their needs are worth a little discomfort. Additionally, there are times when you and they can work through it together and that strengthens your relationship.

6. Discuss the Woman Rules or Man Rules about sex with your children. Building their awareness of the influence the Rules have can give them insight and a glimpse at how they might make their own choices instead of unknowingly adhering to the Rules.

7. Make sure you discuss consent. This is too important of a topic to forget about or avoid.

8. Talk to your partner or coparent about what you would like to discuss with your children. Information about sex and sexuality can be confusing enough on its own, so you want to make sure you are on the same page as any other caregivers who might have a similar discussion with your children.

9. Understand that with all the media access children have today, you may need to consider beginning talking to your children at an earlier age than you expect.

Summary

This meeting was meant to give you real, practical tools for navigating the concepts of sex and physical intimacy yourself, and giving healthy messages to your children, when the timing is appropriate. Thinking back to your own introduction to these concepts is important. Perhaps you are content with how you were first exposed to ideas of sex and physical intimacy. More likely, though, it was not the healthiest introduction and you felt confused, uncertain, and maybe even afraid. Many *adults* don't even have real conversations about these topics, so girls are left to fend for themselves, learning from their peers and the media – less-than-healthy sources of information.

This meeting is designed to set you up for successful conversations and healthy messaging to your children when it comes to sex and all types of intimacy. A major part of that is beginning to consider what you want to talk about when it comes to the "Sex Talk." Starting to think about that now, even if your children are too young or you're not fully ready for the conversations, is one way to begin to decrease the anxiety you likely feel about discussing it. The more you put into this work ahead of time, the more confident you will feel when it comes time to have the Sex Talk and the more likely your children will be to receive it well.

Women's Health

In this meeting, you will explore what it means to be healthy in a holistic way. Physical health can often be overlooked for and by women. However, it is also easy for us to miss some or all of the dimensions of health that impact our lives. That is why this meeting will have you explore eight dimensions of wellness. At the end of the meeting, you will have the opportunity to create your own comprehensive wellness plan so that you can give attention and care to the various needs in your life.

The goals of Meeting 14 are:

1. To explore how moms handle their physical health and wellness needs.
2. To identify barriers and challenges that moms experience when trying to take good care of their bodies, minds, and spirits.
3. To begin creating a Wellness Plan as a way of being intentional about caring for your own needs.

Eight Dimensions of Wellness

"Wellness is a holistic integration of physical, mental, and spiritual well-being, fueling the body, engaging the mind, and nurturing the spirit." – National Institute of Health

Amazing Moms! Motherhood Curriculum, Workbook, First Edition. Sophia Murphy, Dan Griffin, and Harrison Crawford.

What Is Wellness and Why Does It Matter?

There are different ideas about what wellness entails. For the purposes of this program, we chose a model from the National Institute of Health that breaks wellness up into eight dimensions: physical, intellectual, emotional, social, spiritual, vocational, financial, and environmental.

You may be wondering why this attention is being given to physical health and getting care. It is important to understand that there are connections between your experiences as children and young women that influence your physical health over time as you get older. Research shows that there is a connection between the experience of traumatic events and environments in childhood and physical health issues later in life.

Remember the ACE from our previous meeting? That study provided evidence of connections between people's experiences of childhood trauma and future difficulties such as mental health challenges, addiction, and physical health issues. This was an incredibly important moment in our understanding of how our minds and bodies are connected, and the impact that childhood trauma has on the body.

What does that mean for you? Hopefully, it is helpful to you to understand this connection and it emphasizes how important it is for you to seek regular medical care. If you aren't experiencing any concerns at this time, but your score when you completed the ACE questionnaire was four or more, this can encourage you to think ahead about your physical health. This is not meant to frighten you but to remind you of the importance of practicing good physical health as best you can.

Take some time to explore the different dimensions of wellness, as well as the barriers you might face when trying to give attention to each dimension. Identifying examples will give you a list to choose from in the future when you want to do a wellness-related activity. Anticipating barriers ahead of time can help you consider ways to overcome the barriers before you encounter them.

8 dimensions and their definitions were obtained from Stoewen (2017).

Physical: Caring for your body to stay healthy now and in the future.
   Examples:

Barriers:

Intellectual: Growing intellectually, maintaining curiosity about all there is to learn, valuing lifelong learning, responding positively to intellectual challenges, and expanding knowledge and skills while discovering the potential for sharing your gifts with others.
   Examples:

Barriers:

Emotional: Understanding and respecting your feelings, values, and attitudes, appreciating the feelings of others, managing your emotions in a constructive way, and feeling positive and enthusiastic about your life.
   Examples:

Barriers:

Social: Maintaining healthy relationships, enjoying being with others, developing friendships and intimate relations, caring about others, letting others care about you, and contributing to your community.
   Examples:

Barriers:

Spiritual: Finding purpose, value, and meaning in your life with or without organized religion and participating in activities that are consistent with your beliefs and values.
    Examples:

Barriers:

Vocational: Preparing for and participating in work that provides personal satisfaction and life enrichment that is consistent with your values, goals, and lifestyle, and contributing your unique gifts, skills, and talents to work that is personally meaningful and rewarding.
    Examples:

Barriers:

Financial: Managing your resources to live within your means, making informed financial decisions and investments, setting realistic goals, preparing for short-term and long-term needs or emergencies, and being aware that everyone's financial values, needs, and circumstances are unique.
    Examples:

Barriers:

Environmental: Understanding how your social, natural, and built environments affect your health and well-being, being aware of the unstable state of the earth and the effects of your daily habits on the physical environment and demonstrating commitment to a healthy planet.

Examples:

Barriers:

My Physical Health

Physical health is only one aspect of wellness, but one that many moms do not believe they can prioritize. There can be many different reasons for this, but the importance of taking care of yourself physically cannot be overstated. The following questions are meant to get you thinking more about your perspectives on your physical health, your children's physical health, and any changes you are willing to make to be more intentional about taking care of yourself and your children's physical health needs.

To answer the following questions, rate yourself on a scale of 1–5 using the following scale as a guide:

1 = Not much, 2 = A little, 3 = Somewhat, 4 = A good amount, 5 = A great deal

1. On a scale of 1–5, how important is your physical health to you? _____

2. On a scale of 1–5, how well do you care for your physical health? _____

3. On a scale of 1–5, how much do you emphasize physical health and exercise to your children (not solely for physical appearance or attractiveness)? _____

4. On a scale of 1–5, how much do you encourage your children to participate in activities to promote wellness? _____

5. Say a little bit about how/why you chose the numbers you chose to the above questions.

6. What barriers or challenges influence your ability to take care of you and your kids' needs?

7. How can you deal with the barriers and challenges identified above?

8. What do you plan to do to move closer to the scores you want? Please write three specific actions you will take.

   a.

   b.

   c.

Into Action: Complete Your Wellness Plans

Now that you have a better understanding of the different dimensions of wellness, it is time for you to consider what you are interested in working on to improve any of the dimensions. Consider any of the dimensions that you may not have put much thought into before. Or perhaps there were one or two dimensions that you immediately recognized as areas you want to improve in. The creation of a specific plan will help you identify exactly what you want to do to make progress in the area(s) you choose.

The plan itself is meant to be a structured goal-setting plan. You can use this same approach with any type of goal you want to achieve, and the process is broken down for you here:

- Identify a goal and clearly define what the goal is. For example, "get in shape" is too vague – "go to the gym three times a week" is nice and clear.

Another example: "I want to better understand my finances and create a budget."

- Choose specific steps you can take to make progress on the goal. Break your goal down into what needs to be done first. For the gym example, this could be "sign up for gym membership and schedule an orientation with a trainer at the gym."
  - *For budget example*: "I'll sit down and list all my bills out and then my income."
- Decide what timeline you will complete the specific steps. Putting a timeframe on the action steps keeps you moving forward. For the gym example: "I will go to the gym to sign up on Thursday at 9:00 a.m. when I have time off work."
  - *For budget example*: "I'll create the list of bills and income information by Friday."
- Identify anything you need to help you accomplish the goal (for example, support from specific people and/or resources you need). Gym example: "I need a ride to the gym," or "I'm nervous so I would like my friend to come with me."
  - *Budget example*: "I need to get bill statements from a few companies to see what costs I have to deal with," or "My friend is excellent with money, I want to ask her/him for support."
- Consider what obstacles you might run into. This helps prepare you ahead of time versus trying to deal with barriers when they come up. Gym example: "I might not be motivated on Thursday morning, and I might want to postpone going," or "I might be really sore."
  - *Budget example*: "I am scared to learn what my issues with money might be," or "I will feel overwhelmed when I try to do this."
- Try to game plan how to overcome the obstacles you predict might come up. Gym example: "I will reward myself for going to the gym and signing up with (something that's not overly unhealthy)," or "I'll get a heating pad and Epsom salts to help with sore muscles."
  - *Budget example*: "I will use a grounding skill to help ease my anxiety before I do this," or "I will focus just on getting my bills organized before looking into my income and trying to figure out a budget."

You are encouraged to use the Wellness Action Plan worksheet on the next page to really help you set quality goals and work toward the improvements you want to make. This worksheet is a helpful way to stay organized.

Wellness Action Plan:
Create an outline for your wellness goals

Remember the 8 Dimensions of Wellness: Physical, Intellectual, Emotional, Social, Spiritual, Vocational, Financial, Environmental

Goal	First Step	Timeline	Needs	Barriers	Solutions
What will you do? Write down your goal, but also the reason(s) you want to meet this goal, or the "why" of your goal.	What is the first step you need to take? Be as specific as you can.	When are you going to complete your first step? When do you want to complete the entire goal? Be as specific as you can.	What do you need to make this goal happen? Is there anyone who can help?	What is keeping you from reaching this goal? What could happen that would make reaching this goal difficult?	What can you do to take care of the barrier(s) you identified?
Goal 1:					
Goal 2:					
Goal 3:					
Goal 4:					
Goal 5:					

How will you know you have reached your goal? What are the results you want?

Goal 1:

Goal 2:

Goal 3:

Goal 4:

Goal 5:

Practical & Tactical

In the meeting, we talked about how important it is for you to model healthy habits and wellness behaviors for your children. For this Practical & Tactical exercise, you are encouraged to write down three ways you can use your example to get your children involved in wellness.

Consider what you might be able to do to involve them in activities that you do to promote your own health and wellness or come up with creative ways to work on this together. As you think of ideas, write them in the space provided below and then choose a timeframe to do the activities with them. Also, consider the different dimensions of wellness and how you might be able to work on different dimensions with them.

Wellness ideas to practice with your children:

1.

2.

3.

When will you try each of the activities you identified earlier?

1.

2.

3.

Summary

By this point in the program, you have heard numerous times that your children will do what they see you do. You are a role model to them, so modeling healthy choices and habits will increase the chances they make healthy choices and develop healthy habits. Meeting 14 was designed with this idea in mind: help you recognize how you can develop your own well-being so your children pick that up from you. There is an added emphasis on physical health because once again the Woman Rules tend to direct women and moms away from attending to their physical health needs.

Learning to advocate for yourself is a vital step as a woman, especially in spaces where you may be treated poorly, disbelieved, or undermined. It's important that you talk about this so that you don't gaslight yourself or minimize your needs when they occur. When you have negative experiences with medical professionals who don't believe you, you're less likely to listen to your own internal cues, speak up, or seek help again. This creates the pattern of burnout and resentment that was discussed. The only way for you to show up as a healthy mother is to prioritize your own health first. You can't pour from an empty cup.

You deserve to be the healthiest you can be, and your children deserve that from you too!

MEETING 15

Healthy Discipline

This meeting may be intense for you. We know that some people grew up in tough environments while others grew up in violent environments. There is a whole continuum of safety that girls grow up in. Some of you will have had the privilege of feeling safe and loved and valued your whole childhood. Others of you will have had experiences that would literally break some people. And everything in between. This meeting explores the differences between discipline and punishment because of the hugely important roles they play in raising children.

You will have an opportunity to learn about different discipline and parenting styles, which style(s) you use most often, and which one(s) you want to use more intentionally. We then ask you to take a very comprehensive look at abuse and violence in a way that women, or people in general, often do not discuss or explore. Take care of yourself and use the skills you have been learning in case you are triggered. And, as always, talk to someone and get support and help if you feel overwhelmed.

The goals of Meeting 15 are:

1. To define discipline and explore ways to use healthy discipline.
2. To learn how discipline can lead to abuse and violence as a way to exert power and control.
3. To identify how to develop a healthy relationship with discipline, power, and control.

Amazing Moms! Motherhood Curriculum, Workbook, First Edition. Sophia Murphy, Dan Griffin, and Harrison Crawford.

Defining Discipline

The word "discipline" gets used frequently, but many times it is used to describe behaviors that are actually punishment. The differences are very important, so this is an opportunity to separate these two terms and get a better understanding of what they mean.

- *Definition of discipline*: Training that corrects, molds, or perfects. Discipline involves teaching and helping to instill good values. A noble goal of discipline can be to help your children learn "self-discipline" so they can recognize good values and correct, learn, and grow themselves.
- *Definition of punishment*: A penalty for a fault, offense, or violation. Punishment is a negative response to something that is perceived as wrong. Research consistently shows that punishment is less effective than reinforcement (positive responses to good choices or behaviors).

Now that you know the difference between discipline and punishment, feel free to take notes on what healthy discipline and unhealthy discipline look like based on the discussion in this meeting.

- Examples of *healthy* discipline:

- Examples of *unhealthy* discipline:

Parenting Styles

People are unique in how they raise their children, but there are some common styles of parenting that capture most ways that parents try to interact with their children. The following are three common parenting styles, described specifically for moms.

1. *Dictator*: The dictator style (also called authoritarian) is focused on getting children to obey and comply. There is little focus on teaching children

150

self-discipline, problem-solving, or good judgment. Often, moms who use this style set overly strict and rigid rules. Many moms who use this style use harsher punishment techniques, such as spanking or humiliation. One of the difficulties caused by this style is that the children learn to behave appropriately only to avoid punishment, and not because they value good behavior as its own reward. Another downside to spanking can be that children learn it is okay to resolve interpersonal conflict through physical means. It can teach them that it is acceptable to physically hurt someone they love because that is what they experienced.

2. *Lax/Uninvolved*: Moms who practice lax discipline are often inconsistent, do not set firm boundaries with their children, and show little interest in teaching their children discipline or addressing misbehavior. The uninvolved mom may be around, but she is not concerned about what her children do, about correcting their behaviors, or about teaching them self-discipline. Sometimes the mom who uses this style is uninterested in her children's lives. Other times, this type of mom wants to focus more on being the "fun mom" and not having to be the one to correct or hand out consequences to her children. Many other times, the uninvolved mom may be struggling with her own challenges like addiction or mental health needs, keeping her from focusing on healthy discipline.

3. *Firm-but-fair*: The firm-but-fair style (also called authoritative) blends the best aspects of the other two styles. Moms who use this style take a firm-but-fair approach to discipline. Rules, expectations, and consequences for the children are clearly set. However, they are not overbearing and rigid, meaning children are given the freedom to exercise their own judgment and learn lessons on their own. More critically, the rules and expectations are enforced *consistently*, and the children are taught the *reasons* those rules and expectations exist. Most firm-but-fair responses to misbehavior involve discussion, coaching, and exploring different ways the children can behave that do not result in negative consequences for them.

Abuse and Discipline

Many people did not experience *healthy* discipline as children. You may have had caregivers who called what they were doing to you "discipline," but what they were doing was punishment or even abuse. You may have already made a connection in your mind between discipline and abuse. You may have experienced abuse growing up but were taught that the abuse was ok because "you got what you deserved," or it was "teaching you some respect," or it "makes you less dramatic." Not all abuse is an attempt to discipline, and not all discipline is abusive. However, it is important to know the different types of abuse to be more aware of your own actions when it comes to disciplining, and to make sure those actions are not abusive.

Subgroup Discussion Questions: Healthy Discipline

Answer the following questions in your subgroups. Please be mindful of your own reaction to these questions as well as what the moms in your subgroup might be experiencing. Remember to use the tools you have learned to help regulate any trauma reactions, discomfort, fear, anxiety, or other difficult emotional responses.

1. How were you taught discipline as a child? Which parenting style(s) did you experience? Was this style (or styles) effective or ineffective, and why?

2. How were you taught discipline as an adolescent? Which parenting style(s) did you experience then? Did the style(s) change from when you were a child? Was this style (or styles) effective or ineffective, and why?

3. Which parenting style/s do you find yourself using the most? What have you found to be most effective and least effective?

4. How much did culture impact the discipline and parenting style/s you experienced as a child? How much does it impact the type of discipline and parenting style/s you use now?

5. If you have a partner or coparent, how do you coordinate your discipline with him/her/them? If you don't coordinate with another caregiver, what prevents you from doing so?

Subgroup Discussion: Abuse and Discipline

This discussion can be very challenging, so please remember to check in with yourself and use any of the tools you have learned in this program to help calm and regulate yourself if you are feeling triggered, anxious, or any other discomfort. The next set of questions dives further into the topic of abuse, so be mindful of how you are responding as well as how your fellow moms are responding.

Answer the following questions in your small group:

1. What surprised you when you had to come up with examples for each type of abuse?

2. Do you know someone who has experienced any of these types of abuse? Which ones?

3. Have you experienced any of these types of abuse? How did you feel afterward? How do you feel now talking/writing about it?

4. Have you used any of these behaviors on your children? How did you feel afterward? How do you think they felt?

5. What do you think is going on in a mom's head when she uses any of these behaviors on her child? What could that mom do differently beforehand to stop from using any of these behaviors?

Types of Abuse

The following are four common types of abuse, with examples. This is meant purely as a reference moving forward if you ever need/want to remind yourself of the various examples.

1. *Physical abuse*: pinching, slapping, pushing, hair pulling, spitting, restraining, shaking, kicking, choking, dragging, ripping clothing, biting, throwing objects, hitting with objects, slamming doors, kicking doors, punching walls, using one's body to block or intimidate someone, punching, burning, and stabbing.

2. *Sexual abuse*: sexual jokes, harassment, violating another person's boundaries, conveying inappropriate information, inappropriate touching, voyeurism, sexual hugs, commenting about developing bodies, reading or viewing pornography with a child, exhibitionism, fondling, French-kissing a child, oral sex, and penetration.

3. *Emotional abuse*: withdrawing, withholding approval or affection, manipulation through dishonesty, intimidation, and refusing to acknowledge the other's feelings.

4. *Verbal abuse*: name-calling, ridicule, constant criticism, blaming, threatening, and shouting or screaming.

The Gender-Inclusive Power and Control Wheel*

GENDER-INCLUSIVE
POWER AND CONTROL WHEEL

Physical and sexual assaults, or threats to commit them, are often linked to other abusive behaviors. Although physical assaults may occur only occasionally, they can instill the fear of future violence, allowing the abuser to take control of the partner's life. The Gender-Inclusive Power and Control Wheel is a helpful tool to understand the overall pattern of abusive and violent behavior.

Coercion and threats: Making and/or carrying out threats to do something to hurt the partner. Threatening to leave the partner or report the person to welfare. Threatening to make a false accusation.

Intimidation: Making the partner afraid by using threats, looks, and gestures. Destroying the partner's property. Abusing pets. Wielding weapons or kitchen implements.

Gender privilege: Treating the partner like a servant: acting like the "king or queen of the castle." Being the one to define the partner's roles. Making a false allegation.

Emotional abuse: Putting him or her down. Humiliating the person. Playing head games. Not taking responsibility for one's own actions. Ridiculing the partner's appearance or sexual performance.

Economic abuse: Preventing the partner from getting a job, or demanding the partner work longer hours or get a second job. Making the partner ask for money. Not letting the partner have access to family income.

Isolation: Controlling what he or she does, who the partner sees and talks to, what he or she reads, and where the partner goes. Limiting the partner's outside activities. Using jealousy to justify actions.

Using Children: Making the partner feel guilty about the children. Criticizing the partner in front of the children. Telling the children the partner doesn't love them. Interfering with visitation.

Denying, minimizing, and blaming: Making fun of the abuse And not taking his or her concerns seriously. Saying the abuse didn't happen. Shifting responsibility for the behavior. Saying the abuser caused it.

Power and control (center)

Original Power and Control Wheel developed by:
Domestic Abuse Intervention Project
202 East Superior Street
Duluth, MN 55802

Adapted by:
SAVE: Stop Abusive and Violent Environments
Technical assistance - Training - Education
P.O. Box 1221
Rockville, MD 20849
6/24/09

https://www.med.unc.edu/beacon/wp-content/uploads/sites/598/2018/03/GenderInclusivePCWheel.pdf

Amazing Moms! Motherhood Curriculum

Into Action

Answer the following questions. If you feel comfortable doing so, discuss your answers with your partner, co-parent, or a trusted friend.

1. How has your understanding of discipline changed? If it has not changed, describe why.

2. In what ways do you use or teach discipline like your parent(s)? In what ways do you do things differently?

3. What have been the most effective ways you have taught your children discipline?

4. What are some unhealthy discipline behaviors that you are willing to change?

5. How can you improve your coordination with your partner, coparent, or any other caregivers when it comes to teaching discipline to your children?

Practical & Tactical

Spend time talking to your children about discipline. Ask them to explain how they perceive your approach and how effective they feel it is. Some example questions are listed here. Adjust the wording to fit your children's age and developmental level.

- When you make a choice that you know I don't think is ok or I will disagree with, what do I do that's helpful? What do I do that does not help?

- When you make a choice that you know I don't think is ok or I will disagree with, how would you like me to react?

- What do you like about how I react now? What don't you like about it?

- What helps you learn that a choice or behavior is not ok?

- What can I do to help you make good choices as often as possible?

Summary

Before you continue reading this, take a nice, deep breath in through your nose, pause, and exhale it fully through your mouth. Well done. This program covers many difficult topics and conversations, and the discussion of abuse and discipline in this meeting takes a hard look at some challenging information. But being a parent is about having some of these hard conversations! The takeaway of this meeting is that it takes real focus and intention to use discipline in a healthy way and to be able to draw a firm boundary around anything that is abusive.

You may have grown up experiencing some of the same behaviors that were discussed today. We ask you to remind yourself of this: It is not your fault. It's also possible that some abusive behaviors you experienced as a child or adolescent (or even adult) slipped into your own parenting. If that is the case, you need to recognize that those behaviors are now in the past and cannot be repeated. If repairing relationships is needed to leave those behaviors behind, then you have learned some tools to begin the repair process. Sometimes, this might require additional help and support. If that's the case, own that and lean into it. The reward is worth the effort. You have a special opportunity to change for the better. You and your children deserve those positive changes!

As someone committed to being a conscious mother, you now have the information to guide you in your parenting so that you can teach your children discipline in healthy, effective ways. Being intentional about how you teach discipline and how you reward and punish your children is vital to breaking any cycles of violence or abuse that may exist in your history or your current experience. Mistakes will be made, but you now have the tools to limit those mistakes to "minor" ones. You also have the support of your fellow moms in the group and the facilitator(s).

Take care of yourself in the days to come. This meeting has the potential to trigger difficult memories, feelings, and impulses. Rely on the skills you have learned in this program, recognize when you would benefit from the support of others, and most of all remember the reason you are completing this program: to be the best mother you can be. To be an Amazing Mom!

MEETING 16

The Art of Play

After a number of challenging topics, this meeting explores a lighter one: play! How much time have you spent thinking about the importance and benefits of play in your children's lives? This meeting explores the research about the importance of play in the lives of children and adults, and then encourages you to share with and learn from the other mothers in this group. You can work through some questions about the most effective way to play with your kids, and then you get a chance to play! How cool is that? Enjoy.

The goals of Meeting 16 are:

1. To discuss the importance of playing with your children.
2. To share your experiences and successes in playing with your children so everyone in the group can learn from one another.
3. To learn how to use teachable moments during playtime to pass along skills you have learned in this program.
4. To have some FUN with the other moms!

Playtime is great! Playing with your children is something you probably imagined as soon as you found out you were going to be a mom. Even better, playtime has positive

Amazing Moms! Motherhood Curriculum, Workbook, First Edition. Sophia Murphy, Dan Griffin, and Harrison Crawford.
© 2026 Sophia Murphy, Dan Griffin, and Harrison Crawford. Published 2026 by John Wiley & Sons, Inc.

impacts on your children in many ways. Not only that, but playtime is good for you, the mom, as well!

There is a lot of research that recognizes the importance of play for our children's development. According to the American Academy of Pediatrics, "Play allows children to use their creativity while developing their imagination, dexterity, and physical, cognitive, and emotional strength." Children develop a wide range of skills through play: learning to share, dealing with conflict, practicing decision-making, learning about what interests them, and much more. They develop self-confidence and resilience that can help them cope with challenging situations in the future. Play offers physical benefits too: healthier bodies, improved motor skills, and an overall value of being active.

Benefits of Play for Children

- Social skill development
- Physical development
- Helps develop self-control
- Helps develop emotional regulation skills
- Improves imagination
- Begins to teach teamwork
- Improves communication skills
- Improves child's gross and fine motor skills (depending on the activity)
- Helps develop leadership skills
- Reduces stress
- Increases oxytocin – the hormone related to empathy, bonding, and trust; this improves emotional, physical, and social health in children
- Forms closer bond with parents
- Helps develop resiliency – the ability to cope with challenges
- Provides frequent learning opportunities and teachable moments

Benefits of Play for Parents

- Increases oxytocin – the "love" hormone – in parents – helps with bonding, lowers stress, has health benefits
- Bonding with their child

- Gives parents insight into their child's world and mind – interests, feelings, thoughts
- Helps parents improve communication with their child – some children may communicate more effectively through play
- Gives parents insight into how their child might learn best
- Offers teachable moments that can be very helpful to teach new skills – and since it's during play it does not feel tedious to the child
- Gives parents insight into their child's response to success, failure, and obstacles

How Do You Play? Discussion Questions

1. What are your favorite things to do when you play with your children?

2. What do you think are your children's favorite things to do or play with you?

3. When playing with your children, are you more likely to do what they want to do, or what you want to do? Why? Take some time and really think about this before answering.

4. Do you feel you have enough time to play with your children? If not, what's getting in the way?

Teachable Moments Discussion Questions

Playtime is great and the benefits have already been discussed. Part of the benefit of play is the ability for your children to learn important lessons and skills. As their mother, you can, at times, help them recognize some valuable lessons and life skills through your interactions with them during playtime. Read the following scenario and then answer the questions.

Scenario: A mom and her children are playing their favorite board game. Mom pulls off a great move, but a move that hurts one of the kids' chances of winning. The child gets angry, picks up his game piece, and throws it across the room. This is a teachable moment. There are a lot of directions the mom could go with her response, and they all teach her child something slightly different.

- What are some of the ways the mom in this scenario could choose to respond? List any you can think of whether you agree with them or not.

- What are some of the skills we have learned in this program that the mom could try to teach her child?

Tips for Playtime with Your Children

- Actively observe, listen, support, talk, and understand.
- Give plenty of opportunities for the child to lead the play. Don't intrude and try to assert that things be done your way, but still be involved. Let the play be child-driven as often as possible.

- Be emotionally supportive, nurturing, and show your child that you love him/her/them unconditionally. You can do this by being present when playing (e.g. not checking your phone or watching TV).
- It's not about doing fancy things, taking them to all sorts of elaborate activities, spending money – it's about interacting with them.
- Active play (being physically engaged) is more beneficial than passive play (e.g. screen time).
- Have unscheduled and unstructured playtime – free play.
- "If your child is smiling, laughing, or fully engaged with you then you're doing it right."

Into Action: Superhero Logo Project

The following prompts will be used as part of an activity during the final meeting of this program – in which you will create a Superhero Logo. There will be more description of the reasons behind this activity to come, but the goal is to have you use this Superhero Logo to represent yourself and your strengths. Please also involve your children in this exercise, if possible. Talk to them about the three prompts and invite them to help you come up with something or even have them choose some of them.

We want that final activity to be very meaningful to you, which is why you are being asked to work on the prompts below ahead of time. Please take your time to complete them thoughtfully and make sure to bring them to the next meeting.

*** *This is not about your skill at drawing, but rather choosing meaningful symbols.*

1. A drawing/picture of an animal that represents you.
2. A drawing/picture of a symbol of your strength.
3. An image from the most powerful women/moms you respect.

*** *For any of the above, you can choose to print or cut out a picture (e.g. off the Internet or from a magazine) instead of using a drawing. You will also be able to use magazines during the activity in the final meeting.*

Practical & Tactical

Look at your schedule between today and the next meeting. Consciously make time to play with your children each day between now and the next meeting. Even five more minutes than what you usually do is significant, whether that bumps it up to 60 minutes or takes it from no time to 5 minutes.

Write down when you want to make time to play with your children (e.g. when you get home from work, when they get home from school, after dinner, etc.). Ideally, make time to play with each child one-on-one if that is possible. Writing these things down adds power to them and increases the likelihood you will follow through.

Summary

"All work and no play makes Jack a dull boy." This is certainly one thing that the movie *The Shining* got right. It was time to have a little fun in this program! At the same time, you had the opportunity to learn about the benefits of play that go beyond just enjoying yourself and your kids. It's amazing how simply playing with your children is so healthy, both for your children and for you!

It is important to recognize that not every mom is able to spend time with her children right now. If that is your situation, our hope is that this meeting helped highlight the simple joy you can experience through play, and the benefits that you get from engaging in play yourself. Looking into the future, we wish for this meeting to give you hope on your journey to become the mother you want to be for your children. When the time comes that you have the opportunity, play away!

MEETING 17

A Balancing Act

Balance can be a difficult thing to achieve in our lives. You feel stressed by your job, parenting responsibilities, and everything else you must do. This meeting is an opportunity to explore what healthy balance looks like and to understand that it can look different at different times. Complete balance is not possible – and that is okay. Remember, it is about doing it consciously, not perfectly. At the end of this meeting, you will have the opportunity to consider everything you have been learning in this program in a way that works and makes sense for you. We know that it can be overwhelming to have all these different ideas and skills presented in a short period of time. This is your opportunity to not only make it manageable, but also find an effective way to really implement it into your life so that it is truly time well spent.

The goals of Meeting 17 are:

1. To explore the ways you can manage all the competing interests and requirements that come with motherhood.
2. To demonstrate and consider the benefits of having support from others in your life.
3. To create an action plan for how to find balance in a way that fits you as an individual.

Amazing Moms! Motherhood Curriculum, Workbook, First Edition. Sophia Murphy, Dan Griffin, and Harrison Crawford.

Finding Balance

Something you may hear a lot about when it comes to parenting is finding balance. You get all sorts of pressure as a mom about needing to balance your life: Don't let the kids have too much screen time, make sure you have a good job but also that you're not working too much, get your kids into lots of activities to keep them busy but not *so* busy that they are exhausted or burn out. You must also balance having fun with maintaining order and discipline with your children. Perhaps on top of all of that, you feel pressure to work on your relationship with your significant other, or you're single and you want to find time for a relationship. It can all feel overwhelming.

Moms tend to overlook taking care of *themselves* when trying to meet all their obligations. Many moms often don't spend a lot of time thinking about healthy ways to make sure they recharge. And they usually spend even less time actually *doing* those healthy behaviors. The term to use to describe taking time for yourself in healthy ways is "self-care."

Self-care has come up before in this program and refers to specific activities or behaviors that are good for you from a physical, mental, social, or spiritual perspective. In other words, self-care addresses many of the dimensions of wellness that you explored a couple of meetings ago. Like wellness, self-care is an area that women and moms rarely focus on. You may tend to see self-care as selfish and something that takes away from the time and energy you *should* be giving to your children and partners. You also may tend to see self-care in narrow ways such as going to the spa, taking a bath, etc. And just because those are historically feminine activities, they are also stereotypes and not the way that every person finds reprieve or relaxation. However, that stereotype misses the whole point. For one thing, those are *great* activities. But self-care is also much more than that. It is an important part of a balanced and healthy life.

Subgroup Discussions: Finding Balance

It is time to explore this topic for yourself and figure out how you want to define balance. Use the opportunity to discuss these ideas.

1. What does "finding balance" mean to you?

Amazing Moms! Motherhood Curriculum

2. On a scale of 1–5, rate how well you do with balancing all the competing needs you have in your life. Why did you choose that rating?

3. How have your ideas about balance changed since having children?

4. What area(s) of your life do you think could use more attention right now? (*Hint: look back to the Wellness Action Plan you started working on after meeting 14.*) Why did you choose this area/these areas?

Into Action #1: Complete My Amazing Mom Action Plan

Look through the list of topics, concepts, and skills we have covered in the *Amazing Moms!* program so far and choose up to three that are most important to you and that you want to start using or implementing in your life right away.

Step One: List up to three topics, concepts, or skills/tools you want to prioritize:

1.

2.

3.

Step Two: Get more specific – how do you want to use, practice, or implement each of the items you chose?

1.

2.

3.

Step Three: Choose one specific action you commit to doing over the course of the next week to make progress on each item above. Remember, avoid being vague and choose something that will allow you to know when you have completed the task.

1.

2.

3.

Step Four (*save this for the end of the week*): How did you do on your action steps? Did you meet your commitment? If so, repeat this process for either a new set of skills or concepts, or keep the same ones you chose and just take the next step for each one.

Make notes in the following space on how you did over the course of the week on each item, and what your next steps are.

1.

2.

3.

Practical & Tactical #1: Identifying Supports

Support comes in many forms: a significant other, a family member, a friend, a group of other moms, a church group, a recovery group, various mutual support groups, and online support, among others. Take some time to think about the support you have in your life. Also, consider new supports you may want to seek out. Make a list in the space provided, and mark whether the person, group, etc. is a current support or a new one you identified. If it is a support you would like to seek out, briefly describe one step you can take to develop this new support. Over time, try to fill out the whole list so you have ten supports, a combination of ones that are active and others you plan to seek out.

1.

2.

3.

4.

5.

6.

7.

8.

Practical & Tactical #2: Activities for Balance

The following are examples of different behaviors or activities you can do to address different areas of your life. Take time to add your own ideas to the lists over time. The more you add, the more options you have in addressing each area to try and find your desired balance.

1. Create a list of self-care ideas:
   - Take a walk
   - Exercise
   - Read a book
   -
   -
   -
   -
   -
   -

2. Create a list of fun activities to do with kids:
   - Play a board game
   - Color in a coloring book
   - Plan your weekend or time off together
   -
   -
   -
   -
   -
   -

3. Create a list of fun things to do with a friend or significant other:

- Take a walk together
- Have dinner just the two of you
-
-
-
-

4. Create a list of fun things to do as a family. Focus on making them short and simple:

- Take a family walk
- Go to the park
-
-
-
-

5. Other ideas:

-
-
-
-
-
-
-
-
-
-

Summary

You have so many competing interests that are begging you for time and attention; it is enough to drive a mom mad! The aim of this meeting was to improve your ability to manage those competing interests in more effective ways. In our opinion, finding balance is more effective when you take time to evaluate what requires your time, focus, and energy, and then you commit to meeting those demands - in other words, being intentional about what you want to use your energy on. The tasks and responsibilities that require your attention likely change from time to time, so this meeting was designed to help you get a better sense of how to shift focus when needed and prioritize the things that are most important at any given moment. Giving equal time to all required tasks is not a realistic goal, so the ability to shift your attention based on what's needed the time will hopefully help you feel less stressed and more confident in your ability to meet what is being asked of you.

We recognize that this program has been an onslaught of information, tools, activities, and "assignments" for you to practice and complete. We have asked a lot of you! Being a conscious, healthy, and intentional mother can be a lot of work at times. That is why we created the Amazing Mom Action Plan to help you clarify what you feel is most important to you and then choose specific steps you want to take to accomplish what you desire most. Once you feel good about what you have accomplished, you can always come back to this workbook and choose new concepts, skills, and exercises to focus on and practice.

*** *Do not forget to finish the Into Action from Meeting 16 so you are prepared for the Superhero Logo activity that will be part of Meeting 18.*

MEETING 18

Vision of Motherhood

This may or may not be your last group meeting as part of the *Amazing Moms!* program. Either way, it is a powerful point in your journey where you get to really summarize the importance and breadth of the work you have done. You will be introduced to a concept called the "Drama Triangle" that highlights different roles that exist in creating relationships, ones that tend to be more harmful in the long run. You will also have an opportunity to see how to step out of the role(s) you have played and begin to play the role of "Healthy Bad Guy." You have been preparing to create your Superhero Logo for a couple of meetings now based on the prompts from the Into Action activity after meeting 16. Hopefully, you have included your children in the preparation, if possible. Now you get to create your actual Superhero Logo and share it with your fellow group members. Finally, because women are not always the best at saying goodbye or acknowledging their true feelings for someone, you will have the opportunity to honor the connections you have made with the other Amazing Moms in your group in a special way.

The goals of Meeting 18 are:

1. To create a vision of the mother you want to be by creating a personal "Healthy Bad Guy" superhero logo.

Amazing Moms! Motherhood Curriculum, Workbook, First Edition. Sophia Murphy, Dan Griffin, and Harrison Crawford.

2. To acknowledge each other and the hard work and growth that has occurred in this group.

3. To practice healthy closure in your relationships.

The Drama Triangle

Here is a new framework called, The Drama Triangle. The Drama Triangle was proposed by a psychiatrist named Stephen Karpman in the 1960s and offered a perspective of challenging roles that people inhabit when in relationships. He argued that people fall into three roles labeled The Victim, The Rescuer, and The Persecutor. These roles all complement each other in ways that create relationships, however, the roles become more hurtful than helpful over time. As you read on, you'll see a fourth role that exists outside of the triangle and offers an opportunity to avoid the drama.

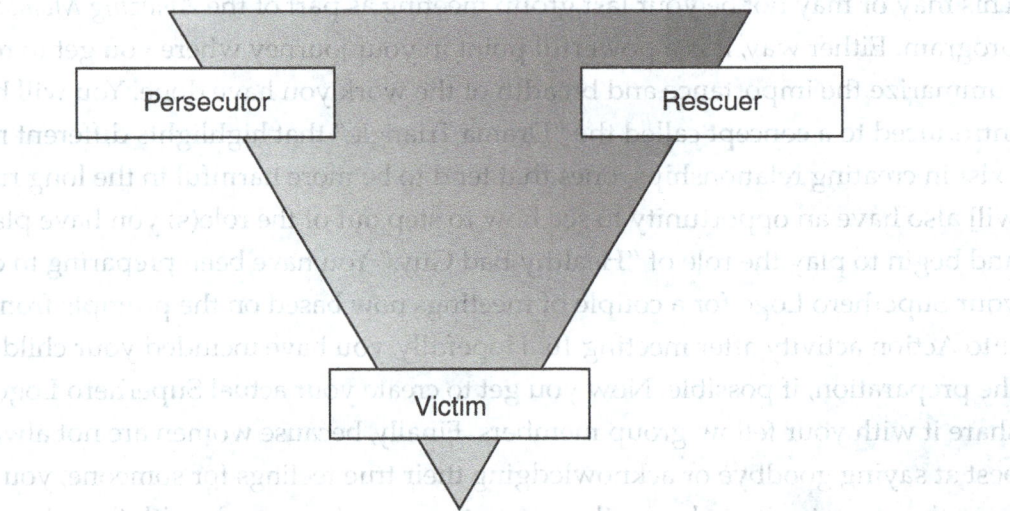

Karpman Drama Triangle from Stephen Karpman (image from wikipedia.org/wiki/Karpman_drama_triangle)

The Three Roles: Victim, Rescuer, Persecutor

- *The Victim*: The victim is someone who sees the world and life as happening *to* them. They are not victims of an actual crime currently; however, they struggle to see their own autonomy and feel helpless and hopeless. They often blame others for what is happening in their life and struggle to take any personal

Amazing Moms! Motherhood Curriculum

responsibility. This can happen in both positive and negative ways. They will put others on a pedestal and attribute anything good in their lives to this other person. They will also see others as the cause of all the pain in their lives. This role often works well in a relationship with a rescuer because the victim subconsciously wants someone else to fix their problems.

- *The Rescuer*: The rescuer is someone who draws a sense of purpose and worth by focusing on others. This person will rush in to fix a problem without ever being asked to do so. This person may also forcibly interject themselves into situations against the wishes of others because the rescuer believes they know better. The rescuer enjoys the sense of being "needed" and only feels good about themselves when receiving recognition for all they've done. However, the rescuer will get tired and become upset trying to maintain this role. They are prone to keeping score and creating tallies that other people don't know about. When they want their generosity reciprocated, they will accept nothing less than what they perceive is fair. It's common for rescuers to pair well with a victim until the rescuer is burned out. Then the rescuer may shift to the victim role and wonder why no one is there *for* them and only takes *from* them.

- *The Persecutor*: The persecutor often struggles to engage with others because this person sees themselves as above others. The persecutor will be the first person to tell others what they are doing wrong and how they could do things better, specifically to meet the standards set by the persecutor. A rescuer may become a persecutor when the victim in their life doesn't accept the rescue that's being offered. To keep the other person in the victim's role, the persecutor may shame the victim for making a "poor choice." The persecutor may also push people away by staying in a place of judgment.

Important Concept: The Healthy Bad Guy

The Healthy Bad Guy is the fourth role in Karpman's framework and is someone who refuses to play the game of the drama triangle and refuses to be pulled into any of these roles. By definition, this role exists *outside* of the triangle and offers an alternate way to be in relationship with others without the drama. This can only happen with self-awareness, self-healing, and a host of new skills – skills like the ones you have been learning in the *Amazing Moms!* program! To engage with people in their lives in a mindful and intentional way, the Healthy Bad Guy relies on vulnerability, assertive communication, flexible boundaries, and healthy conflict. They only look like the Bad Guy to people in the other roles in the triangle. They may receive negative feedback from those still stuck in the other roles and may feel pressure to even return to old dynamics to stay within the relationships. It takes courage to stay outside the lines. This is what makes them a true superhero.

Healthy Bad Guy Superhero Logo

Please use the logo that you think is best as provided by your therapist or your group facilitator.

Summary A

If you have completed all the meetings for **Amazing Moms!** *in order, please continue below. If you have only completed part of the program and plan to continue with the meetings you have not yet gone through, please skip to Summary B below for the summary for meeting 18.*

What a long, amazing journey this has been! Take a moment to reflect on everything you have gone through to complete this *Amazing Moms!* program. . .

This final meeting was designed as an opportunity for you to express how hard you have worked to be an Amazing Mom. The Superhero Logo activity was a chance for you to present your vision of yourself as you step into being the mother you want to be. You can take pride in what you created, and we hope you keep it as a symbol of the work you did and the progress you made.

Equally as important was the opportunity to share your feedback with the other moms in the group. All of you worked so hard over the course of the program, and the connections you made here are ones that are probably unlike any others you have had to this point. We want you to cherish those connections and recognize the special group of women and moms you were a part of.

Please jump to page the Congratulatory Page for more wrap-up information.

Summary B

If you have not yet gone through all the meetings and you are continuing in the **Amazing Moms!** *Program after completing Meeting 18, please see the summary below:*

Meeting 18 is the technical end point of this program. However, you may not have gone through each meeting in order, and if that is the case, you are encouraged to continue and go through the materials you have yet to explore.

In Meeting 18, you learned about the concept of the Drama Triangle and the roles that are associated with it. You had an opportunity to consider which role(s) you have played in past and present relationships, but then you were shown how they can become harmful over time. That brought you to the concept of the Healthy Bad Guy – the person, in your case the mother, who discards those limiting roles and decides not to "play the game" of the Drama Triangle. This person is only a "bad guy" in the eyes of others who are stuck in the three roles of the triangle. However, as someone who has been practicing more self-awareness, vulnerability, and healthy boundaries, you now have the opportunity to embrace the Healthy Bad Guy role that will allow you to be the Amazing Mom you strive to be.

Also in this meeting, you finished creating your Superhero Logo. This activity was a chance for you to present your vision of yourself as you step into being the mother you want to be. You can take pride in what you created, and we hope you keep it as a symbol of the work you did and the progress you made.

As you continue to go through the other meetings in the *Amazing Moms!* program, please remind yourself of the phrase we use so often in this work: It's not about doing things perfectly, it's about doing things consciously.

Congratulations on Finishing the *Amazing Moms* Program!

Thank you for the time and effort you invested. As the authors, we are honored to have committed mothers such as you, experience everything that *Amazing Moms!* has to offer. We sincerely hope that this experience has helped you learn about yourself and the mother that you want to be. We also hope that you feel confident in your own abilities to use the information you learned, and that you will continue to see the benefits from your experience in this program.

Your journey to be the best mother you can be doesn't end here, but you have achieved a huge milestone in that journey. Now it is up to you to continue learning, growing, listening, and teaching others. If you have friends who are also mothers, offer to share your experience and lessons learned with them. You can be an ambassador for helping the mothers around you grow in similar ways to you, if they want to, though remember that not everyone is ready to dive into this work just yet.

Please note that there is a QR code on the next page that will take you to a survey where you can give us feedback on your experience. We sincerely want to hear from you, so please check that out. You can find more resources and information related to AmazingMoms!andyourjourneytoconsciousmotherhoodonourwebsite,www.amazing-moms.com. We also encourage you to come back to this workbook over time to refresh

Amazing Moms! Motherhood Curriculum, Workbook, First Edition. Sophia Murphy, Dan Griffin, and Harrison Crawford.
© 2026 Sophia Murphy, Dan Griffin, and Harrison Crawford. Published 2026 by John Wiley & Sons, Inc.

your memory, refresh your skills, and remind you of all the hard work you put into bettering yourself!

Once again, congratulations on taking a huge step in your journey as a conscious mother and an Amazing Mom, and please remember: it's not about using your skills perfectly, it's about using them consciously.

After Completing This Program

As the creators of *Amazing Moms!*, we value information on how the program impacts your life and your growth as a mother. With that in mind, we would be very grateful if you could take just a few minutes to answer some questions to give us your feedback on the experience you had.

Simply scan the QR code below and you will be directed to a brief survey.

We appreciate any feedback you can provide because we want to continue improving the *Amazing Moms!* program for future participants. Your honest opinions are of great value to us and will help shape future editions of this curriculum for all the Amazing Moms to come.

Amazing Moms! Motherhood Curriculum, Workbook, First Edition. Sophia Murphy, Dan Griffin, and Harrison Crawford.
© 2026 Sophia Murphy, Dan Griffin, and Harrison Crawford. Published 2026 by John Wiley & Sons, Inc.

Relaxation and Grounding Exercises

Here, you will find all the grounding and relaxation exercises that are included in the *Amazing Moms!* program. This section can be a great resource for you to return to when you find yourself needing a refresher on these skills. This is also a good resource for you to come to in times you want to choose an exercise and you can decide what fits your needs in the moment. The exercises are shown here in the same order they were introduced in the meetings.

Box Breathing

This exercise can help you calm your body and your mind quickly and efficiently:

1. Put one hand on your chest and the other on your stomach.

2. As you take a few breaths, notice which hand is moving more. Try moving your breath deeper into your lower abdomen so that your hand on your stomach moves more as you breathe.

3. Close your mouth and press your tongue lightly to the roof of your mouth. Let your jaw relax.

4. Take in a full breath slowly through your nose, counting to four.

Amazing Moms! Motherhood Curriculum, Workbook, First Edition. Sophia Murphy, Dan Griffin, and Harrison Crawford.
© 2026 Sophia Murphy, Dan Griffin, and Harrison Crawford. Published 2026 by John Wiley & Sons, Inc.

5. Hold your breath, counting to four.

6. Exhale all the air through your mouth, counting to four.

7. Rest for a count of four.

8. As thoughts come up, acknowledge them, and then return your focus to your breathing and counting.

9. Go through three more rounds of this breathing on your own, slowly breathing in through your nose for four counts, holding for four counts, breathing out through your mouth for four counts, and resting for four counts.

Palms Up, Palms Down

This exercise can help you move aside anything that is weighing on your mind, or even any physical discomfort, in order to allow you to focus your mind on the present.

1. Sit up straight in your seats, with both feet on the floor and your eyes focused on your hands.

2. Hold both your arms outstretched, with your palms side by side and facing up as if someone was about to put something in your hands. Make sure you don't rest your arms on anything; they should be out in front of you in the air.

3. Visualize any thoughts, feelings, and stresses bothering you right now.

4. Now, imagine placing all of your stresses, problems, troubles, and anything bothering you into your hands. These emotions and thoughts are out of your bodies and lying in your hands. Picture them there.

5. Go back inside yourself and find any remaining pain, discomfort, and stress. Then slowly feel these sensations move out through your arms and into your hands.

6. Imagine the weight of holding all these problems, difficult thoughts and emotions, and physical distress in your hands. Feel the strain of carrying them and the weight pushing down on your hands.

7. Now, slowly turn your hands upside down, letting your palms face the floor. Let all the problems, stresses, difficult feelings, and negativity fall to the floor. For now, drop your burdens.

All these problems have not disappeared or been resolved, but you have chosen to put them down for the time being to be able to focus on what you need to in the present moment.

Amazing Moms! Motherhood Curriculum

In with the Good Breathing

Get comfortable in your seat. Concentrate on your breathing. Focus on your breath in, a pause, and your breath out. Feel your body expand outward with each full inhale and then return back to the center with each full exhale. With each breath, breathe a little deeper and move your breathing further down into your abdomen.

As you breathe in, take in positive things such as hope, courage, and love. As you breathe out, expel the challenging things you don't want in your life such as stress, self-doubt, and anxiety. Do this exercise for two minutes. Remember, breathe in the good and the positive, and breathe out the bad and the negative.

Five Senses Mindfulness

The Five Senses Mindfulness exercise is a simple and effective way to practice being in the present moment, in the "here and now." Find a quiet place where you can practice this for about 5–10 minutes without interruption. As you go through the steps, take about 15–30 seconds in between to give yourself time to experience each sense.

1. *Hearing*: Spend a few moments focusing on what you hear. Notice the different sounds, perhaps ones you didn't hear initially. Suspend any judgment of them. They are neither good nor bad; they just are.
2. *Smell*: Shift your attention to any smells you pick up. Again, notice them without assigning any judgment of good or bad, just that they are.
3. *Touch*: Focus on your sense of touch. Notice the feeling of the fabric of your clothes, or wherever your hands are resting. Notice the sensation of sitting in the chair, your feet on the ground.
4. *Sight*: Concentrate on your sense of sight by just observing what is around you. There are many things you could notice, from the different shades of color to different textures of the objects around you. Avoid judging the sights and just observe them and then move to the next one.
5. *Taste*: Shift your attention to your sense of taste. If you have a snack, feel free to take a small bite. If not, notice any taste inside your mouth now, or the taste of the air you're breathing, again suspending judgment.

Place of Peace Relaxation Exercise

1. Take a deep breath in while you silently count to four. One, two, three, four.

2. Now, breathe out slowly, silently counting to four again. One, two, three, four.

3. Remember to breathe from your abdomen. Breathe in again. One, two, three, four.

4. And out again. One, two, three, four.

5. Now, picture in your mind a place of peace. Maybe you have been there before or maybe it is a place of your dreams. Maybe it's your bed or a comfortable chair. Maybe it's sitting by a lake or lying in the sun by the ocean. Maybe it's a special place you visited as a child or a scene from one of your favorite movies. It may be a real place or an imaginary place. See that place in your mind.

6. Keep breathing slowly and deeply.

7. Let the muscles in your face relax.

8. Let your brow relax.

9. Let your jaw relax.

10. Let your neck and your shoulders relax.

11. Imagine all the tension draining out of them. Let it go.

12. Let your hands and arms go limp next to you.

13. Let your middle relax – your chest and your abdomen.

14. Keep breathing in and out.

15. Let your hips and your legs relax.

16. Let your feet relax.

17. Relax your whole body and imagine yourself in that favorite, safe place. This is your place of peace. You are safe in this place. Your life is the life you always wanted it to be. You are the loving and caring father you want to be.

18. Your life is full of peace. You are full of peace.

19. As you breathe these next couple of times, breathe in the word "peace."

20. As you breathe out, exhale all the pain from your past and all the negative feelings and thoughts.

21. Breathe in peace.

22. Breathe out pain.

Repeat the breathing process several more times.

Exercise: Gratitude Breathing

Take a minute or two to identify three things you are grateful for in this moment. They do not need to be "huge" things. Even the small things are worth your gratitude. Write these three items down here:

1.

2.

3.

Next, make yourself comfortable and prepare to do some deep breathing:

- Take a deep breath through your nose, pause, and exhale fully through your mouth.
- Repeat this again.
- Now, with each full breath you take in through your nose, pause and say one of your gratitude items to yourself either out loud or in your mind.
- After you state your gratitude, exhale your breath fully through your mouth.
- Take another full breath through your nose, but this time as you pause with your full breath in, say another one of your gratitude items to yourself.
- Exhale the full breath through your mouth.
- Repeat this a third time, saying your third gratitude item to yourself before you exhale fully.
- Take a couple of minutes to repeat this same process until you have repeated each of your gratitude items three times.

    Practicing gratitude can help build resilience. Even thinking about small things you are grateful for helps strengthen your "resilience muscles." Writing them down adds another layer to the positive effect that this can have.

    This can also be turned into a cool activity to practice with your children. Have them practice gratitude – getting them to develop this habit now can have a big payoff throughout their lives!

Eagle's Wings Exercise

1. Take a few deep breaths from down in your abdomen.
2. Next, cross your hands across your chest so the tips of your middle fingers are just below your collarbone. The rest of your fingers will lay relaxed on your upper chest.
3. Try to have your fingers pointing up instead of outward. You can interlock your thumbs if this helps make it easier.
4. Now, slowly and steadily alternate tapping your hands on your chest repeatedly: right, left, right, left, resembling the flapping wings of an eagle.
5. Continue to take slow, deep breaths and continue tapping steadily
6. Notice what is going through your mind and body: whether it be thoughts, images, feelings, or physical sensations
7. Notice these things coming and going as you would watch clouds passing in the sky.
8. Continue breathing slowly and deeply.
9. Continue tapping: right, left, right, left, right, left.
10. When you feel in your body that you are relaxed, grounded, and it has been enough, you may stop.

Loving Kindness Meditation

1. Get into a relaxed position, for example, seated or lying down.
2. Take a deep breath through your nose.
3. Hold it.
4. Now, slowly let it go through your mouth.
5. Let's do that one more time, please.
6. Take a deep breath through your nose.
7. Hold it.
8. Now, slowly let it go through your mouth.
9. Continue breathing deeply, slowly, and steadily.
10. Focus on feeling kindness toward yourself. Move past any thoughts of doubt that come up.

11. Say the following phrases to yourself, not out loud but in your head.

    a. May I be happy.

    b. May I be healthy.

    c. May I know peace.

12. Continue breathing slowly and deeply.

13. Now, think of a relationship you have struggled with. Picture that person in your mind.

14. Imagine that person as a child, before you knew them, before any conflict with them.

15. Say the following phrases to the image of this person you have in your mind:

    a. I wish you to be happy.

    b. I wish you to be healthy.

    c. I wish you to know peace.

16. Continue breathing deeply and slowly, breathing in kindness, and breathing out pain and conflict.

Full Body Breathing

Begin in a standing position, making sure you have space in front of you for this exercise.

- Standing up straight, take a deep breath in for six counts through your nose. One, two, three, four, five, six.

- Hold your breath for a count of four. One, two, three, four.

- Exhale your full breath through your mouth for six counts. One, two, three, four, five, six.

- Now, slowly bend forward at the waist, keeping your knees slightly bent, and let your arms dangle down toward the floor. Bend as far as you are comfortable with.

- As you inhale slowly and deeply, return to a standing position by rolling up slowly, lifting your head last. Do this over the course of six counts.

- When you reach your full standing position, hold your breath for a count of four.

- Exhale slowly as you return to your starting position, bending forward from the waist. Do this for six counts.

- Repeat the process again. Bend at the waist, with your arms dangling toward the ground. Slowly take a deep breath and roll up to a standing position over six counts.
- Hold your breath for a count of four at the top.
- Exhale slowly as you roll back down to your starting position over six counts. Now, go through this routine two more times on your own. Make sure to do this slowly to help avoid any pain or injuries. Notice how it feels to stretch while you breathe.

OPTIONAL: If you have any pain issues, especially in your back, the following can be a less physically demanding version of the exercise.

- Start with your arms hanging down against your sides.
- As you begin to take a deep breath in for a count of six, slowly raise your arms in an arc until they meet above your head outstretched. The motion is similar to doing a jumping jack.
- Hold your breath and your arms outstretched for a count of four.
- As you exhale for a count of six, bring your arms down along the same arc until they are back at your sides.

This exercise combines the physical element of stretching with the same breathing skills as some of the other exercises. It is a good exercise to do in the morning to help stretch out stiff muscles and open your breathing passages.

Progressive Muscle Relaxation

The exercise involves tensing different muscle groups. If you have pain in any area of your body and you feel that tensing that area would be painful, skip the tension part of that muscle group and focus on the relaxation of the muscles.

1. Begin by taking a deep breath for a count of four. Notice the feeling of air filling up your lungs. One, two, three, four.
2. Hold your breath for a count of four. One, two, three, four.
3. Release the breath slowly for a count of four and let the tension out of your body. One, two, three, four.
4. Pause for a count of four. One, two, three, four.

Amazing Moms! Motherhood Curriculum

5. Even slower now, take another deep breath this time for a count of six. One, two, three, four, five, six.

6. Hold it for a count of six. One, two, three, four, five, six.

7. Slowly release the breath over a count of six, feeling the tension leaving your body. One, two, three, four, five, six.

8. Now, move your attention to your feet. Begin to tense your feet by curling your toes and the arch of your foot. Hold the tension and notice what it feels like. *(Five-second pause.)*

9. Release the tension in your feet and notice the new feeling of relaxation.

10. Next, shift your focus to your lower legs. Tense the muscles in your calves. Hold them tightly and pay attention to the feeling of tension. *(Five-second pause.)*

11. Release the tension from your lower legs. Again, notice the feeling of relaxation. Remember to continue taking deep breaths.

12. Next, tense the muscles of your upper leg and pelvis and hold it. You can do this by squeezing your thighs together. Make sure you feel tension without going to the point of strain. *(Five-second pause.)*

13. Now, release and feel the tension leave your muscles.

14. Begin to tense your stomach and chest. You can do this by sucking in your stomach. Squeeze harder and hold the tension. *(Five-second pause.)*

15. Release the tension. Allow your body to go limp. Notice the feeling of relaxation.

16. Continue taking deep breaths. Breathe in slowly, noticing how it feels as the air fills your lungs.

17. Release the air slowly, feeling it leave your lungs on its way out.

18. Next, tense the muscles in your back by bringing your shoulders together behind you. Hold them tightly. Tense them as hard as you can without straining and keep holding. *(Five-second pause.)*

19. Release the tension from your back. Feel it slowly leaving your body, being replaced by a feeling of relaxation. Notice how different your body feels when you allow it to relax.

20. Tense your arms all the way from your hands to your shoulders. Make a fist and squeeze all the way up your arm. Hold it. *(Five-second pause.)*

21. Release the tension from your arms and shoulders and notice how your arms feel limp and at ease.

22. Move up to your neck and your head. Tense your face and neck by distorting the muscles around your eyes and mouth. *(Five-second pause.)*

23. Release the tension. Again, notice the new feeling of relaxation.

24. Finally, tense your entire body. Tense your feet, legs, stomach, chest, arms, head, and neck. Tense harder, without straining, and hold that tension. *(Five-second pause.)*

25. Now, release and allow your body to go completely limp. Pay attention to that feeling of relaxation and how different it is from the feeling of tension.

26. Begin to wake your body up by slowly shifting your arms and legs.

Holding tension in the muscle and then releasing it often gives a good sense of the feeling of full relaxation in that muscle. By going through all the major muscle groups, you can practice removing the tension from the whole body. Additionally, shifting your focus to different parts of your body is a grounding practice by keeping your mind in the present – the "here and now" – and noticing sensations in your body. As you practice this exercise, you will likely see an improvement in your ability to really feel the relaxation effect.

REFERENCES

Administration for Children and Families (n.d.). What is Historical Trauma? Resource Guide to Trauma-Informed Human Services. https://www.acf.hhs.gov/trauma-toolkit/historical-trauma-concept

American Psychological Association (n.d.). Resilience. Psychology Topics. https://www.apa.org/topics/resilience

American Psychological Association. (n.d.). Trauma. https://www.apa.org/topics/trauma

American Society of Addiction Medicine (2019, September 15). Definition of Addiction. Quality of Care. https://www.asam.org/quality-care/definition-of-addiction

Black C. Chapter One: Getting to Know Trauma In Unspoken Legacy. In: *Addressing the Impact of Trauma and Addiction Within the Family*. Central Recovery Press, 2018: 8–9.

Brown, Brené (2013, January 15). Shame vs. Guilt. Brene Brown. https://brenebrown.com/articles/2013/01/15/shame-v-guilt/

Centers for Disease Control (2021, April 6). About the CDC-Kaiser ACE Study. Violence Prevention. https://www.cdc.gov/violenceprevention/aces/about.html

Conflict styles [handout]. (n.d.). Adapted content from Hall, J. (1969). Conflict management survey.

Fletcher, J. (2022). *Trauma-Informed Healing for LGBTQIA+ Communities [Recorded Presentation]*. Arizona Trauma Institute: Mesa, AZ, United States

Ginsburg KR, The Committee on Communications, & The Committee on Psychosocial Aspects of Child and Family Health. The Importance of Play in Promoting Healthy Child Development and Maintaining Strong Parent-Child Bonds. *Pediatrics* 2007; **119**(1): 182–91. https://doi.org/10.1542/peds.2006-2697.

Karpman, S.B. (2015). Karpman drama triangle. https://karpmandramatriangle.com/index.html

Loepkky, J. (2023, August 2). Purity Culture and Its Effect on Mental Health. Verywell Mind. https://www.verywellmind.com/purity-culture-impacts-mental-health-7564315

Murphy, S. (2023). Orgasms 101. TBD Health.

(n.d.). Feelings Wheel. FeelingsWheel.com. https://feelingswheel.com/

(n.d.). Protective and Compensatory Experiences (PACEs). University of Oklahoma. chrome-extension://efaidnbmnnnibpcajpcglclefindmkaj/https://www.ou.edu/content/dam/Tulsa/ecei/docs/ACEs%20and%20PACEs%20questionnaires.pdf

Positive Psychology (2019, March 23). 23 Resilience Building Activities & Exercises for Adults. Resilience and Coping. https://positivepsychology.com/resilience-activities-exercises/#science-based-activities

Psychology Today (n.d.). Intergenerational Trauma. https://www.psychologytoday.com/us/basics/intergenerational-trauma

The Rape Abuse and Incest National Network (RAINN) (n.d.). Sexual Assault. https://rainn.org/articles/sexual-assault

Rhoton, R. and Aubrey, T.E.R. (2019). Transformative care: a trauma-focused approach to caregiving.

SAVE: Stop Abusive and Violent Environments (2009, June 24). Gender-Inclusive Power and Control Wheel. https://www.med.unc.edu/beacon/wp-content/uploads/sites/598/2018/03/GenderInclusivePCWheel.pdf

Shegog ML. Medical gaslighting of women is real and so is its toll. *D.C Journal*. 2023. https://dcjournal.com/medical-gaslighting-of-women-is-real-and-so-is-its-toll/#:~:text=%E2%80%94Seventy%2Dtwo%20percent%20of%20women,prove%E2%80%9D%20their%20symptoms%20to%20doctors.

Shore, J. (2019, December 9). Rape Culture in America. Focus For Health Foundation https://www.focusforhealth.org/rape-culture-in-america/

Smiler, A. P. (2016). Consent: giving it and receiving it. In Dating and Sex: A Guide for the 21st Century Teen Boy (pp. 93). Essay, Magination Press

Stoewen, D.L. (2017). Dimensions of wellness: change your habits, change your life. *The Canadian Veterinary Journal* 58 (8): 861–862. https://pmc.ncbi.nlm.nih.gov/articles/ PMC5508938/

Substance Abuse and Mental Health Services Administration (2024, November 8). Mental Health. Center for Mental Health Services. https://www.samhsa.gov/mental-health

[Ted-Ed]. (2013, July 19). Listening to shame - Brené Brown [Video]. YouTube. https://www.youtube.com/watch?v=7jtZdSRst94

United Nations Population Fund (n.d.). What is Bodily Autonomy? https://www.unfpa.org/sowp-2021/autonomy